·8 0· G R E A T
N A T U R A L
H A B I T A T
P L A N T S

·80· GREAT
NATURAL
HABITAT
PLANTS

KEN DRUSE

CLARKSON POTTER/PUBLISHERS
NEW YORK

Published by Clarkson N. Potter, Inc., 201 East 50th Street, New York, New York 10022. Member of the Crown Publishing Group.

Random House, Inc. New York, Toronto, London, Sydney, Auckland
http://www.randomhouse.com/

The photographs in this book were previously published in *The Natural Habitat Garden* by Ken Druse.

CLARKSON N. POTTER, POTTER, and colophon are trademarks of Clarkson N. Potter, Inc.

Printed in China

Design by Maggie Hinders and Lauren Monchik

Library of Congress Cataloging-in-Publication Data
Druse, Ken.
80 great natural habitat plants / Ken Druse.— 1st ed.
1. Native plants for cultivation—United States.   2. Natural landscaping—United States.   I. Title.
SB439.D65   1998
635.9'51—dc21   97-20884

ISBN 0-609-80085-X

10 9 8 7 6 5 4 3 2 1

First Edition

Acknowledgments

I want to thank some of the people who helped produce this book: Chip Gibson, President and Publisher of Crown Publishers; Lauren Shakely, Clarkson Potter's Editorial Director, who suggested this project and made the idea into reality; Maggie Hinders, the series designer, and Lauren Monchik, who designed this book; Mark McCauslin, production editor; and Joan Denman, production manager.

I also want to thank Laurie Stark, Joan De Mayo, Tina Constable, Wendy Schuman, and Mary Ellen Briggs for always doing more than their share on our projects. Thanks to Helen Pratt, my indefatigable agent; Ann Kearney-Dutton, photo librarian; Louis Bauer for his patience; and George Waffle for his friendship and efforts. I also must thank Ruth Clausen, whose help in making this book accurate was useful and invaluable.

Lastly, I have to thank you. As I travel and lecture around the country, I see new plants in gardens every day, and gardeners often tell me that my books have inspired them. It is gratifying to learn that my books have helped (and touched) so many.

Contents

Introduction

Before I wrote *The Natural Habitat Garden*, I listened to many presentations on restoring thousand-acre plots of wetland or grassland, and I visited many native plant lovers whose "gardens" were tangles of brush featuring the latest rescued rarity. I can appreciate the rare native, but I also know that you can't sell an idea on merit alone. No matter how noble, an idea must be made friendly, understandable, and beautiful. That is what inspired *The Natural Habitat Garden*, a guidebook to the ways native plant gardens can be useful, beautiful, and ecologically sound.

One possible starting point for a natural habitat garden is what my coauthor, Margaret Roach, and I called a "biohedge." If you are selecting shrubs for a visual screen or even a foundation planting, native ones that provide shelter and food in the form of fruit, nectar, seeds, and nuts can replace the mock-orange and yews that bloom briefly and offer few meals for wildlife.

In the last few years, scores of native plant nurseries have sprung up to provide an enormous variety of plants from which to choose. Almost any wild plant you might want to grow can now be found at a local or mail-order nursery. It is important to make sure that the nurseries propagate their formerly wild offerings and never appropriate them from their natural homes. Most reputable nurseries will state in their catalogs that the plants are propagated. If you are in doubt, ask, but there is an easy way to discover the truth. If a native plant seems too inexpensive to be truly nursery propagated, for example, then it is probably not. No mail-order nursery in the United States is propagating the threatened pink ladyslipper orchid (*Cypripedium acaule*). If you see this for sale, you can be sure it has been wild-collected.

Collecting, or stealing, an endangered plant from the wild is reprehensible. But you can rescue a plant threatened by imminent development, as long as permission has been given by the property owner beforehand. As development encroaches more and more on wild and semi-wild areas, some native plants have become threatened with extinction. At least if we grow a native plant from a reliable source—including from the rescuers—and learn to grow it well, it

will be preserved in our gardens. If gardeners just turned a tenth of an acre over to native plants, there would be a net gain of a million acres for wildings. There can be no more noble gift a gardener can give back to the earth. Try organizing a group of plant rescuers in your area; you might be able to interest the local newspaper in reporting on your efforts.

Obviously, we all are not going to go native overnight. I, for one, am not going to ban all exotic plants—ones from other countries—from my own garden. But I'm making other plantings—especially in the outer areas of my property—purely with indigenous plants. In my new garden in New Jersey, I have collections of plants from all over the world, but when you cross the quiet branch of the river that runs through this property, you enter "New Jersey." This is my indigenous plant garden, an idea borrowed from Dr. Richard Lighty, an inspirational teacher, plantsman, and gardener. In this area I am a purist—all the plants will be from a ten-mile radius of my property, but North American native plants grow in all the gardens I am making. One reason is that they are beautiful. Another is that I think that all gardeners must also be conservators.

80 Great Natural Habitat Plants is a helpful handbook to take with you when you go to the nursery and out to the backyard. I have included information about how North American plants interrelate to form plant communities that you may simulate in your gardens, which will serve not only you and the plants, but the animals that dwell nearby. Although I cannot guarantee that planting the host plants will attract birds or other animals, I do know the results can be remarkable.

The Natural Habitat Garden presented four general conditions in North America, based mostly on rainfall: grassland, wetland, dryland, and woodland. This handbook takes a closer look by presenting plants for community types and the animals—four- and two-legged—who use them. There is a chapter on meadow and prairie plants; one on wildflowers of the woodland; another on plants for the water's edge; and finally, a chapter on plants that have ornamental seed pods and berries. You may be surprised to see some familiar plants from the perennial border, but many more of these plants will not be familiar. In this holistic approach, you will find candidates to make your garden more beautiful, as well as plants to serve the animals who stop in your garden, to sip nectar or bathe by the waterside. Ultimately, you will be helping the natural habitat garden, too, by providing a good home for the native plants—one where they will live long and flourish.

Plants for Meadow and Prairie

Plants for Meadow and Prairie

Some of the most popular plants in English perennial borders—Michaelmas daisies, beebalm, penstemon, for example—first called North America home. These are wonderful flowers of the prairies and meadows that went to Europe for their pedigree as acceptable garden plants. And yet they have been a part of North America's herbaceous (nonwoody) stock that forms an undulating layer of one- to six-foot plants from the wet meadows of Maine to the short-grass prairie of the Dakotas to California's chaparral.

When most people picture wildflower meadows, they imagine fields of sprightly buttons of color, but there are precise definitions for the general plant community types known by these names. A meadow occurs as one step in the succession process of open land in areas that have substantial rainfall. Abandoned farm fields and pastures or burned woodlands begin to come back to life with grasses and non-grass flowering plants—called forbs—started from airborne seeds and seeds dropped by small land animals and birds. In a short time, the seedlings of woody plants begin to poke up through the brush. Soon, the growing shrubs shade out the herbaceous sun-lovers, then the tree seedlings grow into saplings, and the shrubs, too, fade. Finally, after fifteen to twenty years, the woodland emerges.

A prairie is not like that at all. A prairie is a kind of grassland that could be called a "climax community." It is at the last stage of its evolution. The process does not go beyond the prairie because of natural forces: it is too windy for trees to get a foothold, or too dry; it may be too cold in the winter and too hot in the summer; and there may be fires, started by lightning igniting the dried "fuel" in autumn, that not only do not harm the grasslands, but refresh them.

One way to bring the magnificent beauty of these two plant communities to your garden is to give up a bit of the lawn and turn it over to a prairie-style planting in dry areas, or a meadow-style planting in areas of the country where there is more rain. Soon, the birds and butterflies will come to sip nectar and to glean the seeds and fruits, bringing remarkable color, sights, and sounds to the planting.

Allium cernuum
(nodding onion)

Andropogon ternarius
(split beard bluestem)

Asclepias tuberosa
(butterfly weed)

RIGHT
Agastache foeniculum
(anise hyssop)

AGASTACHE FOENICULUM

PRONUNCIATION: ag-as-TASH-ee foe-NIK-ewe-lum

COMMON NAME: Anise hyssop, giant blue hyssop

HOMELAND: Prairies of central North America

HARDINESS: USDA Zones 3–9

SIZE: To 3' tall; 18"–24" across

INTEREST: In summer, dense 4"-long pokers with countless, tiny purplish blue flowers; stiff, branched stems above aromatic, soft, toothed foliage

LIGHT CONDITIONS: Full sun to light shade

SOIL/MOISTURE: Average to poor soil, with good drainage

DESCRIPTION: Anise hyssop is a valuable biennial or short-lived perennial plant in both tallgrass and short-grass prairie communities. It is often seen accompanied by black-eyed Susans, purple coneflowers, asters, and goldenrods, as well as many prairie grasses. The copious seeds provide food for birds; the flowers attract bees, butterflies, and hummingbirds. The fragrant leaves are used for herbal tea. Chew one flower for a taste of sweet licorice. Self-seeds freely. Colorful hybrid agastaches are becoming popular as ornamentals, particularly for wildlife gardens and where water conservation is important.

ALLIUM CERNUUM

PRONUNCIATION: al-EE-um SURN-ewe-um

COMMON NAME: Nodding onion

HOMELAND: Dry, rocky slopes, and in less harsh conditions from New York to South Carolina, and west to the Pacific Ocean

HARDINESS: USDA Zones 4–8

SIZE: 1'–2' tall; 9"–12" across

INTEREST: In summer, umbels of up to 30 bell-shaped, ½" lilac-pink flowers, open on strong scapes, above loose clumps of grayish green, straplike leaves

LIGHT CONDITIONS: Full sun to light shade

SOIL/MOISTURE: Well-drained soil of average fertility

DESCRIPTION: The common name refers to the umbel of flowerbuds, which nod atop the scape. As the buds open, the scape straightens out and becomes S-shaped. Nodding onions drop their seeds freely but colonize slowly depending on the surrounding competition. They are effective among grasses and forbs, and are suitable for transition areas, such as where prairie meets woodland. Useful in ornamental perennial plantings, perhaps in front of earlier-blooming *Baptisia australis* and later-blooming milkweeds. Ornamental in seed as well as in bloom.

ANDROPOGON TERNARIUS

PRONUNCIATION: an-DROH-poh-gon ter-NAIR-ee-us

COMMON NAME: Split beard bluestem

HOMELAND: Prairies, savannas, and meadows of the eastern United States to Kansas, and Florida to Texas

HARDINESS: USDA Zones 6–9

SIZE: 1'–1.5' tall, with flower stems to 4'; plants 1.5' across

INTEREST: Dense clumps of green or purplish green leaves, topped by erect, cottony white flower spikes which remain on the plants for several months

LIGHT CONDITIONS: Full sun to very light shade; tolerant of seaside conditions

SOIL/MOISTURE: Fertile to average soil, well drained or even on the dry side

DESCRIPTION: Split beard bluestem is excellent in prairie or savanna plant communities as a companion for asters, coneflowers, heliopsis, and goldenrods, and other prairie grasses. Planted in a mass it controls erosion effectively on slopes and banks. Colonizes readily. The thick plants provide good cover for birds, and the seeds are a favorite food for sparrows, juncos, and other species. This plant has a future as an ornamental for gardens—especially for its display of seed heads in winter.

ASCLEPIAS TUBEROSA

PRONUNCIATION: as-CLEE-pee-us tu-ber-OH-sa

COMMON NAME: Butterfly weed

HOMELAND: Dry prairie communities of eastern and central North America

HARDINESS: USDA Zones 3–9

SIZE: 2'–3' tall; about 2' across

INTEREST: Upright clumps, with grayish green oval leaves and flat-topped clusters of brilliant orange flowers in mid-summer

LIGHT CONDITIONS: Full sun to very light shade

SOIL/MOISTURE: Average to poor soil, very well drained or even dry

DESCRIPTION: Butterfly weed, along with grasses and asters, is an essential plant for dry, sunny prairie or exposed meadow areas. Its deep taproot enables it to tolerate these conditions readily, but makes transplanting difficult. The vibrant flower clusters attract monarchs, fritillaries, and other butterflies foraging for nectar. Monarchs use the foliage for larval food and the adults pollinate the flowers. After flowers fade, slender, light brown pods appear; these enclose quantities of seeds equipped with silky plumes, which aid in their dispersal by wind. Butterfly weed is gaining in popularity as an ornamental.

Aster lateriflorus
(calico aster)

Chasmanthium latifolium
(northern sea oats)

Coreopsis tinctoria
(calliopsis)

LEFT
Echinacea purpurea
(purple coneflower)

ASTER LATERIFLORUS

PRONUNCIATION: ASS-ter lat-er-i-FLOR-us

COMMON NAME: Calico aster

HOMELAND: Dry to moist meadows and prairies of the eastern and midwestern United States, and south to Florida and Texas

HARDINESS: USDA Zones 4–8

SIZE: 2'–4' tall; 2'–2.5' across

INTEREST: Countless ½" flowerheads, with bright, rosy disk-shaped flowers ringed by short, stubby, pale lavender-pink rays, in fall

LIGHT CONDITIONS: Full sun to light shade

SOIL/MOISTURE: Deep fertile or average soil with good drainage; tolerates dry soil when established

DESCRIPTION: Deep-rooted calico aster is excellent on the edge of meadows and in transition areas where soil may be rocky and moisture scarce. In spite of the small size of the individual flowers, their sheer number produces a dazzling effect for several weeks. The flowerheads are borne on bushy, upright plants clothed with dark green, often purple-tinged foliage. After the blooms are spent, the seed heads persist, and are a source of food for seed-eating birds.

CHASMANTHIUM LATIFOLIUM

PRONUNCIATION: kas-MAN-thee-um lat-ih-FO-lee-um

COMMON NAME: Northern sea oats, inland sea, river oats

HOMELAND: Rich woodlands and savannas of eastern, central, and southern North America

HARDINESS: USDA Zones 5–9

SIZE: 2'–3' tall; 1'–1.5' across

INTEREST: An upright slender grass with dangling, flattened, 1" green flower spikes in late summer, which mature to copper and turn tan in late fall

LIGHT CONDITIONS: Full sun to light shade; partial shade in hot regions

SOIL/MOISTURE: A wide range of soils, provided there is moisture available

DESCRIPTION: Northern sea oats has bright green 6"-long, ¾"-wide leaves, which mature to a coppery brown and turn tan in late fall. The flower spikes are lightly borne on arching stems and remain attractive through the winter, especially when lightly dusted with snow. Excellent in damp woodland clearings or beside shaded streams where suitable companions include late-blooming asters, black-eyed Susans, ironweed, and swamp sunflowers. It colonizes slowly, depending upon the competition. The seeds provide winter food for many species of birds. Northern sea oats is becoming a popular ornamental garden plant.

COREOPSIS TINCTORIA

PRONUNCIATION: ko-ree-OP-sis
tink-TOR-ree-a

COMMON NAME: Calliopsis, dyer's coreopsis,
plains coreopsis

HOMELAND: Meadows and moist prairies from
Minnesota west to Washington, and south to
Louisiana and California

HARDINESS: Annual

SIZE: 6″–36″ tall; 12″–15″ across

INTEREST: Yellow to maroon, sometimes bicolored 2″ daisy flowers on branched stems for
most of the summer

LIGHT CONDITIONS: Full sun to very light
shade

SOIL/MOISTURE: Average to poor soil with
good drainage

DESCRIPTION: This underused prairie annual self-seeds freely where conditions are suitable, making it ideal for meadows and rough fields. It is also useful as a cut flower. It is a regular component of many wildflower seed mixes, and is a source of yellow or burnt orange dye. The seed heads are popular with seed-eating birds.

ECHINACEA PURPUREA

PRONUNCIATION: ek-in-AY-see-a pur-pewr-
EE-a

COMMON NAME: Purple coneflower

HOMELAND: Prairie and savanna areas across
central and eastern United States

HARDINESS: USDA Zones 3–9

SIZE: 2′–4′ tall; 1.5′–2′ across

INTEREST: Showy purplish pink daisy flowerheads, 4″–6″ across, top strong stems all
summer; bristly, hairy, dark green foliage

LIGHT CONDITIONS: Full sun to light shade

SOIL/MOISTURE: Soils of average fertility,
although excessively wet or dry soils are not
appropriate

DESCRIPTION: The attractive flowerheads are composed of a coppery brown central disk, raised in the center and surrounded by drooping, purplish pink ray petals. An essential component of meadow and prairie flora, purple coneflowers are nectar plants for several species of butterflies, including red admirals; the seed heads provide food for chickadees, cardinals, and other bird species. Easy to grow, purple coneflowers are also popular as ornamentals; selection has resulted in several cultivars, including purplish pink 'Bright Star' and 'Magnus', and white-flowered 'White Swan'. If deadheaded regularly, blooming can continue well into the fall.

Eschscholzia californica
(California poppy)

Eupatorium maculatum
(Joe-Pye weed)

Helenium autumnale
(sneezeweed)

RIGHT
Gaillardia pulchella
(annual blanket flower)

ESCHSCHOLZIA CALIFORNICA

PRONUNCIATION: esh-SHOLT-zee-a
kal-if-ORN-ik-a

COMMON NAME: California poppy

HOMELAND: Well-drained sandy areas of
California

HARDINESS: Annual

SIZE: 12″–18″ tall; 6″–10″ across

INTEREST: Bowl-shaped, vivid orange flowers,
to 4″ across, over ferny blue-green foliage in
spring

LIGHT CONDITIONS: Full sun

SOIL/MOISTURE: Sandy, neutral to alkaline
soil, with free drainage

DESCRIPTION: Easy-to-grow California poppies paint the hillsides with bright orange, frequently accompanied by blue or purple lupines. The blossoms twirl closed on cloudy days. Plants self-seed freely, and are regularly included in wild-flower seed mixes. Deep-rooted and difficult to move, they bloom quickly from seed in response to spring rains and complete their life cycle before the searing dry heat of summer.

EUPATORIUM MACULATÚM

PRONUNCIATION: yew-pa-TOR-ee-um
mak-yew-LAY-tum

COMMON NAME: Joe-Pye weed

HOMELAND: Damp thickets, meadows, and
tallgrass prairie communities from New
England to British Columbia, south to North
Carolina and New Mexico

HARDINESS: USDA Zones 2–9

SIZE: 4′–7′ tall; 3′ or more across

INTEREST: Clumps of leafy, speckled stems,
topped with large, flattish clusters of dusty
purple flowerheads from late spring to fall

LIGHT CONDITIONS: Full sun

SOIL/MOISTURE: Moisture-retentive or wet
soil of average fertility

DESCRIPTION: The erect stems of Joe-Pye weed are interrupted with whorls of coarse, oval leaves that are toothed along the edges. The rayless ¼″ flowerheads, though discreet individually, cluster into wide, showy inflorescences. Joe-Pye weed is a natural companion for ironweed, swamp milkweed, and the earlier-blooming blue flag iris, as well as for sedges and grasses. Popular in informal damp positions beside streams and ponds, where its architectural stature can be admired.

Gaillardia pulchella

PRONUNCIATION: guy-LARD-ee-a pull-KEL-la

COMMON NAME: Annual blanket flower, Indian blanket

HOMELAND: Dry plains and roadsides from Colorado and Nebraska to New Mexico, east to Florida, and north along the coast to Virginia

HARDINESS: Annual

INTEREST: Daisy flowerheads, to 2" across; reddish brown disk, brilliant red rays, often yellow-tipped, from mid-summer until frost

SIZE: 12"–20" tall; 12"–15" across

LIGHT CONDITIONS: Full sun

SOIL/MOISTURE: Average to poor, well-drained soil, even on the dry side

DESCRIPTION: Annual blanket flower blooms in about 3 months from seed. Self-seeds in spring and often produces another flush of flowers later. The domed seed heads attract seed-eating bird species. This plant is at its best in a community with Texas bluebonnets, Indian paintbrush, Mexican poppies and others adapted to similar habitats. Blanket flowers are popular as ornamentals in hot summer climates. Hybridization programs have resulted in superior cultivars such as the all red, double-flowered 'Red Plume'. Annual blanket flower or Indian blanket displays the colors of the cloth for which it is named.

Helenium autumnale – *Birds*

PRONUNCIATION: hell-EEN-ee-um aw-tum-NAH-lee

COMMON NAME: Sneezeweed, Helen's flower

HOMELAND: Along streams, in meadows, and in other damp places throughout much of North America from Quebec south to Florida and west to Arizona and British Columbia

HARDINESS: USDA Zones 3–9

SIZE: 4'–5' tall; 2'–3' across

INTEREST: In late summer and early fall, branched, flattish clusters of bright yellow daisy flowerheads bloom on tall stems

LIGHT CONDITIONS: Full sun to very light shade

SOIL/MOISTURE: Moisture-retentive average to fertile soil

DESCRIPTION: The flowerheads are composed of a gently domed, light greenish brown disk surrounded by stubby ½" golden rays which droop slightly. The erect stems have "wings" from the leaf bases. The seed heads, which become dark tan in fall, provide food for several species of seed-eating birds, such as juncos and sparrows. Cultivars bloom earlier or later than the species, with red, copper, orange, and bronze ray flowers. The dried leaves were once ground as a substitute for snuff, hence one common name; some say the plant was named for Helen of Troy.

Hydrangea arborescens
'Annabelle'
(wild hydrangea)

Limnanthes douglasii
(meadow foam)

Lilium superbum
(Turk's-cap lily)

LEFT
Liatris ligulistylis (meadow
blazing star)

HYDRANGEA ARBORESCENS 'ANNABELLE'

PRONUNCIATION: hy-DRAN-jee-a ar-bor-ESS ens

COMMON NAME: Wild hydrangea or hills of snow 'Annabelle'

HOMELAND: Of garden origin. The species grows in shaded woodlands from southern New York to Missouri, and south into Mississippi and Florida.

HARDINESS: USDA Zones 3–9

SIZE: 3'–5' tall and as wide

INTEREST: A dense mounding shrub, crowned in summer with numerous ball-shaped white flower heads, to 12" across

LIGHT CONDITIONS: Full sun to light shade

SOIL/MOISTURE: Fertile soil, with plenty of organic matter added to help retain moisture

DESCRIPTION: The showy flowerheads of 'Annabelle' are composed of countless, mostly sterile, double, creamy-white flowers. These are enhanced by the mass of medium green oval leaves which grow to 6" long. In fall the brownish yellow foliage sets off the spent flowerheads, which dry to a light tan color. 'Annabelle' is a popular, easy-care deciduous shrub for residential gardens. Prune in early spring—may be cut down to 6" for large flowers. Underplant with spring-blooming green 'n gold or wild geranium, or plant with native ferns such as Christmas or Ostrich fern.

LIATRIS LIGULISTYLIS = Bird seed !

PRONUNCIATION: lye-AT-riss lig-yule-i-STY-lis

COMMON NAME: Meadow blazing star

HOMELAND: Usually found in low, damp places in prairie communities from Wisconsin south to Colorado and northern New Mexico

HARDINESS: USDA Zones 3–8

SIZE: 3'–3.5' tall; 1.5'–2' across

INTEREST: Bottlebrush wands of small, brilliant purple flowerheads, red in bud, in mid-summer to fall

LIGHT CONDITIONS: Full sun

SOIL/MOISTURE: Average soil with good drainage, but not excessively dry

DESCRIPTION: Growing from a corm, meadow blazing star makes bushy clumps of stems clothed with grassy leaves. The flowerheads lack ray flowers; they are composed of all disk flowers and open from the top down. Meadow blazing star is an ideal companion for other prairie plants such as culver's root and showy goldenrods, which bloom at about the same time, and for grasses including little bluestem and prairie dropseed. The flowers provide nectar for several species of butterflies, particularly monarchs. In fall, the seeds are a favorite food for goldfinches.

LILIUM SUPERBUM

PRONUNCIATION: LIL-ee-um soo-PER-bum
COMMON NAME: Turk's-cap lily
HOMELAND: Moist meadows from New York and New Brunswick south to Georgia and Alabama
HARDINESS: USDA Zones 3–8
SIZE: 3'–5' tall; 1' across

INTEREST: Elegant, strong stems, with whorls of glossy leaves; umbels of nodding, bright orange flowers
LIGHT CONDITIONS: Full sun to light shade
SOIL/MOISTURE: Damp acid soil, enriched with humus

DESCRIPTION: The orange-red 4" flowers, each borne on an ascending stem, are strongly reflexed, revealing a green throat and heavy maroon spotting inside; the prominent, curved stamens are exserted. Each stem may carry 20–30 flowers. A natural companion for meadow grasses, sedges, and wildflowers such as blazing stars and lobelias. Spreads slowly, by producing young bulbs from the mother bulb, which results in good-sized stands. Plant in fall.

LIMNANTHES DOUGLASII

PRONUNCIATION: lim-NAN-theez doo-GLAS-ee-eye
COMMON NAME: Meadow foam, poached egg plant
HOMELAND: Seasonally wet meadow communities of coastal southern Oregon and California, and the foothills of the Sierra Nevada
HARDINESS: Annual

SIZE: 12"–15" tall; about 12" across
INTEREST: Masses of solitary, 1" 5-petaled yellow and white flowers in spring, above light green, fern-like 5" leaves
LIGHT CONDITIONS: Full sun to very light shade, especially in hot areas
SOIL/MOISTURE: Cool, moist soil of average fertility, but not soggy

DESCRIPTION: Meadow foam, sometimes called poached egg plant, makes broad stands where the conditions are suitably wet. It is found growing with damp-loving rushes and sedges, weaving among them, as well as with California poppies and Pacific Coast mallows. It self-seeds; a fall crop of flowers results from seeds dropped in spring. Attractive to many pollinating insect species.

Lupinus benthamii
(spider lupine)

Marshallia graminifolia
(Barbara's buttons)

Milium effusum 'Aureum'
(golden grass)

RIGHT
Monarda punctata
(horsemint)

Lupinus benthamii

PRONUNCIATION: loo-PINE-us
BEN-tham-ee-eye

COMMON NAME: Spider or Bentham's lupine

HOMELAND: Southern California and north to
the lower Central Valley, on dry hillsides in
the foothills of the mountains

HARDINESS: USDA Zones 8–10

SIZE: 1'–3' tall; 2'–2.5' across

INTEREST: Upright spikes of brilliant blue pea
flowers above clumps of compound, narrow-
fingered, gray-green leaves, in spring

LIGHT CONDITIONS: Full sun

SOIL/MOISTURE: Poor rocky soils that drain
freely

DESCRIPTION: Spider lupine refers to the spidery leaves which are separated into very thin segments and are covered with soft hairs, to reduce water loss through transpiration. The ½" pea flowers are light or dark blue; the standard, or back petal, is splotched with yellow. The seedpods are 2" or more in length; it self-seeds. Good for dry, rocky hillsides, with California poppies and owl's clover as companions. Sometimes grown in ornamental gardens as an annual.

Marshallia graminifolia

PRONUNCIATION: mar-SHALL-ee-a gram-in-
ee-FO-lee-a

COMMON NAME: Barbara's buttons

HOMELAND: Moist pine barrens and savannas
from Pennsylvania south to Florida

HARDINESS: USDA Zones 7–10

SIZE: 6"–18" tall; 10"–12" across

INTEREST: Solitary lavender-pink flowerheads
on slender stems, in summer through early
fall

LIGHT CONDITIONS: Full sun to light shade

SOIL/MOISTURE: Moisture-retentive soil of
average fertility

DESCRIPTION: Often found growing in the wild with mosses and ferns, lobelias, turtleheads, and other moisture lovers. They lack the disk flowers typical of other members of the daisy family; they may reach 1½" or so across. The identity of "Barbara" in the common name remains a mystery.

MILIUM EFFUSUM 'AUREUM'

PRONUNCIATION: MIL-ee-um eff-FYOO-sum

COMMON NAME: Golden grass, golden wood millet

HOMELAND: Damp, shaded woodlands and meadows from eastern Canada to Maryland and Illinois; 'Aureum' is of garden origin

HARDINESS: USDA Zones 6–9

SIZE: Foliage clumps 6"–18" tall; 1'–2' across

INTEREST: In late spring, airy golden panicles of flowers to 2' or more above loose clumps of evergreen, 12" golden leaves

LIGHT CONDITIONS: Light shade

SOIL/MOISTURE: Average, moisture-retentive soil

DESCRIPTION: Cool-season golden grass holds its color on the new growth until the weather becomes hot. It brightens shaded woodland areas and has become a popular ornamental for residential gardens. Plants grown from seed exhibit the golden color. Combine it with spring-blooming green 'n gold, which picks up the yellow in its flowers, or use it as an underplanting for the tall spires of late-blooming snakeroot; it is also attractive with ferns.

MONARDA PUNCTATA

PRONUNCIATION: mon-AR-da pung-TAY-ta

COMMON NAME: Horsemint, spotted or plains beebalm

HOMELAND: Sandy prairie and savanna communities from Long Island south to Florida and Louisiana

HARDINESS: USDA Zones 5–10

SIZE: 6"–24" tall; 1'–2' across

INTEREST: In summer, spikes with whorls of hooded, purple-spotted yellow flowers, circled by showy, pinkish lavender pointed bracts

LIGHT CONDITIONS: Full sun

SOIL/MOISTURE: Soil must be sandy, free-draining, or even on the dry side

DESCRIPTION: Horsemint grows in clumps of square, erect stems. The flower spikes are borne on the upper third; under favorable conditions the bracts are very colorful. Flower spikes last for several weeks and the flowers attract several butterfly species. The dark green, toothed leaves are fragrant and are used for herbal tea. This short-lived perennial or biennial seeds itself, but colonizes slowly. It is suitable for tallgrass or meadow prairie communities, alongside black-eyed Susans, annual blanket flower, and grasses. It is sometimes planted in ornamental native plant and wildlife gardens, and in herb gardens.

Oenothera speciosa
(showy pink
evening primrose)

Physostegia virginiana
(obedient plant)

Ratibida pinnata
(prairie coneflower)

LEFT
Muhlenbergia rigens
(deer grass)

MUHLENBERGIA RIGENS

PRONUNCIATION: myoo-len-BER-jee-ah rih-GENZ

COMMON NAME: Deer grass, grass meadow muhly

HOMELAND: Assorted habitats in Texas, Southern California, and northern Mexico

HARDINESS: USDA Zones 7–9

SIZE: 3'–4' tall; 3' or more across

INTEREST: Evergreen clumps of fine-textured, gray-green leaves. Showy, cordlike panicles of grayish flowers rise above in early summer; these mature to light tan.

LIGHT CONDITIONS: Full sun to partial shade

SOIL/MOISTURE: Adapted to a wide range of soils, but best in well-drained, fertile soil, with moderate moisture. Tolerates drought, heat, and alkaline conditions.

DESCRIPTION: Deer grass retains its foliage color even under drought conditions. The slender flower spikes, which persist for several months, are erect when young, but tend to relax as they age. Deer grass is considered to be a cool-season grass since most of its growth is put on during the fall, winter, and spring. It is valuable massed to control erosion on slopes and coastal sites, especially in harsh western climates. It is a popular specimen plant for ornamental gardens, particularly where water is scarce.

OENOTHERA SPECIOSA

PRONUNCIATION: ee-no-THE-ra spee-see-OH-sa

COMMON NAME: Showy pink or showy white evening primrose, pink sundrops

HOMELAND: Dry fields and prairie communities, and along roadsides from Kansas and Missouri to Texas and Mexico

HARDINESS: USDA Zones 5–8

SIZE: 8"–24" tall; 18" across

INTEREST: In late spring and early summer, showy, pale pink cup-shaped flowers bloom in the upper leaf axils

LIGHT CONDITIONS: Full sun to open shade

SOIL/MOISTURE: Soil of average fertility, well drained or dry

DESCRIPTION: Where conditions are suitable, showy evening primrose colonizes by underground stolons. It makes broad sweeps of grayish green, softly hairy leaves, which are almost hidden by the 1"–2" flowers, which open during the day and close at night. Tolerates dry conditions and root competition well, which is one way to curb its roving habits. Effective in ornamental gardens, especially in hot, dry areas, and in containers.

PHYSOSTEGIA VIRGINIANA

PRONUNCIATION: fy-so-STEE-ja
vir-JIN-ee-ah-na

COMMON NAME: Obedient plant, false
dragonhead

HOMELAND: Wet woods and prairie communities of the Northeast to South Carolina and
west to Texas

HARDINESS: USDA Zones 3–9

SIZE: 3′–4′ tall; 2′–3′ across

INTEREST: Tall, slender spikes of bright pink
flowers in late summer, at the top of
branched, square stems, and above pairs of
lance-shaped leaves

LIGHT CONDITIONS: Full sun

SOIL/MOISTURE: Slightly acid, well-drained,
fertile soil

DESCRIPTION: The close-set individual flowers of obedient plant are 2-lipped, about 1½″ long, and range from pale to deep purplish pink. The plants form clumps above stoloniferous roots, which colonize readily even in heavy clay soils. An essential component of moderately dry meadows and damp spots in prairie gardens, obedient plant is a fine companion for horsemint, beebalms, and grasses. Its popularity as an ornamental and cut flower has resulted in several cultivars on the market; white-flowering 'Summer Snow' and long-blooming, lilac pink 'Bouquet Rose' are widely available.

RATIBIDA PINNATA

PRONUNCIATION: rat-IB-id-a pin-AH-ta

COMMON NAME: Prairie coneflower, yellow
coneflower, drooping coneflower

HOMELAND: Prairies and fields from southern
Ontario to the Dakotas, south to Arkansas,
and west to Georgia

HARDINESS: USDA Zones 4–8

SIZE: 4′–6′ tall; 2′–3′ across

INTEREST: Masses of striking, large yellow
flowerheads with dark brown raised central
disks; blooms for several weeks in mid-
summer

LIGHT CONDITIONS: Full sun

SOIL/MOISTURE: Dry or moist soils of average fertility. Excellent on heavy clay soils.

DESCRIPTION: The flowerheads are composed of an oblong, ½″ to ¾″-high central disk surrounded by strongly reflexed golden ray flowers up to 2″ long. The tall stems are branched above and bear deeply cut, lance-shaped leaves. In fall the seed heads provide food for several species of birds. This is an important member of prairie communities, growing with purple coneflowers, other daisies, and grasses, especially on very heavy clay soils.

Silphium perfoliatum
(cup plant)

Solidago spp. (goldenrod)

Veronicastrum virginicum
(Culver's root)

RIGHT
Rudbeckia subtomentosa
(sweet black-eyed Susan)

RUDBECKIA SUBTOMENTOSA

PRONUNCIATION: rud-BEK-ee-a sub-TOE-men-tos-a

COMMON NAME: Sweet black-eyed Susan, sweet coneflower

HOMELAND: Lush mesic and upland prairies from Indiana to eastern Nebraska, south to Louisiana and Texas

HARDINESS: USDA Zones 4–8

SIZE: 4'–6' tall; 2'–3' across

INTEREST: Upright clumps with individually stalked 2½"–3" flowerheads; features raised reddish brown cones and yellow rays in late summer and fall

LIGHT CONDITIONS: Full sun

SOIL/MOISTURE: Fertile, moisture-retentive soil; tolerates heavy clay well

DESCRIPTION: Sweet black-eyed Susan has handsome, softly hairy, and often thrice-cut leaves. It is found growing with prairie lilies, blazing stars, purple coneflowers, goldenrods, and many species of grasses. Several flowerheads grow on branched stems. They are a softer yellow than other species of rudbeckia and have an anise scent. A good butterfly plant, and the seed heads provide food for seed-eating birds.

SILPHIUM PERFOLIATUM

PRONUNCIATION: sil-FEE-um per-fo-lee-AH-tum

COMMON NAME: Cup plant

HOMELAND: Moist areas of prairies, open woodlands, and meadows of South Dakota to Ontario and south to the Gulf

HARDINESS: USDA Zones 3–10

SIZE: 4'–8' tall; about 2' wide

INTEREST: Flattish clusters of 3"-wide yellow flowerheads in mid-summer to early fall

LIGHT CONDITIONS: Full sun

SOIL/MOISTURE: Soil of average fertility that does not dry out excessively

DESCRIPTION: Bold and imposing, cup plant gets its name from the cup that forms where the opposite, triangular, or oval leaves join at the four-angled stem. Birds and butterflies come to drink here when rainwater has collected; hummingbirds also visit. The seeds are a favorite food for goldfinches. A suitable companion for Culver's root, rattlesnake master and other prairie wildflowers and grasses, moisture-loving swamp rose mallow, and Joe-Pye weed.

SOLIDAGO SPP.

PRONUNCIATION: so-li-DAY-go

COMMON NAME: Goldenrod

HOMELAND: Coastal, meadow, and prairie communities from New England south to Florida and west to Texas, depending upon species

HARDINESS: USDA Zones 3–10

SIZE: 1′–6′ tall; 1′–3′ across

INTEREST: Countless tiny flowerheads with yellow ray flowers arranged in plumes, wands, or flat-topped clusters, in summer and fall

LIGHT CONDITIONS: Full sun

SOIL/MOISTURE: A wide range of soils, from wet to dry and poor to fertile

DESCRIPTION: There are numerous species of goldenrod, and where their natural ranges overlap, they interbreed. They are an important nectar source for butterflies late in the season, and they provide food for seed-eating birds. Several species spread freely by underground stolons; others are clump formers. Goldenrods are natural companions for asters and grasses. As an ornamental they have been spurned in U.S. gardens until recently, perhaps because they were erroneously blamed for being allergenic. *Solidago* actually has heavy pollen, which is rarely wind-borne. Several shorter or more clump-forming cultivars such as 'Crown of Rays' and 'Golden Fleece' have reached the market in the last few years.

VERONICASTRUM VIRGINICUM

PRONUNCIATION: ve-ro-ni-KAS-trum vir-JIN-ik-um

COMMON NAME: Culver's root, bowman's root

HOMELAND: Damp meadows, prairies, and woods of the eastern United States and Canada

HARDINESS: USDA Zones 3–8

SIZE: 4′–6′ tall; 3′–4′ across

INTEREST: Slender, elegant spires of tiny icy blue or white flowers above dark green, leafy clumps in mid- to late summer

LIGHT CONDITIONS: Full sun or partial shade

SOIL/MOISTURE: Best in well-drained, fertile soil containing moisture-retentive organic matter

DESCRIPTION: Culver's root makes neat, erect clumps. It is a beautiful plant both in foliage and in flower. The 2″–4″-long, pointed leaves are toothed and arranged in whorls of 5, at 2″–3″ intervals up the stem. The dense racemes of flowers may reach 9″ in length. A suitable companion for grasses, obedient plant, and red milkweed, as well as species that thrive on drier ground such as prairie coneflower and bee-balm. Excellent in meadows and transition areas between open fields and light woods.

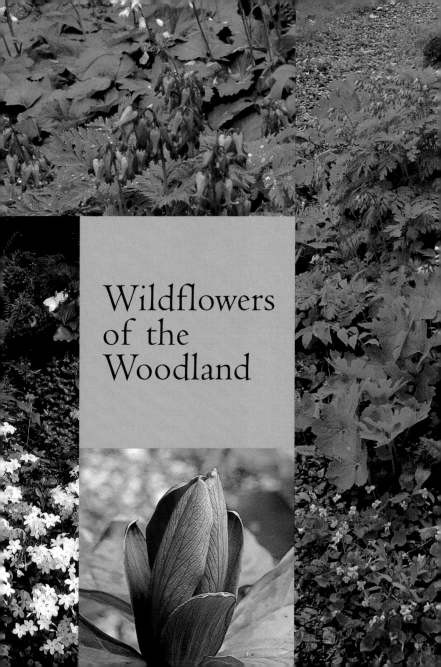

Wildflowers
of the
Woodland

Wildflowers of the Woodland

In the hierarchy of the woodland, the leafy canopy formed by the tall trees is at the top. Then comes the understory of small trees and shrubs, which in turn shelters the forest floor. In this cool, moist, and quiet habitat dwell some of the most subtle but exquisite plants of the botanical kingdom—the woodland wildflowers.

Many of these flowers bloom in spring, and are in fact often called ephemerals because they sprout, shoot up, bloom, set seed, and sometimes even fade away before the last leaves of the deciduous trees fully emerge. In this group are the magnificent trillium with its distinctive three-lobed flowers and the Virginia bluebell (*Mertensia virginica*), with flowers that turn pink, then blue in early spring.

Naturally, a woodland garden needs woods. If trees are not already a feature of your microhabitat—your garden—

you are unlikely to have the right conditions for woodland plants in your lifetime. (It takes a tree several decades to reach its mature height and wingspread.) Many people have trees on their property, however, often with nothing below them but a patch of thinning grass or moss. Since this same location in nature abounds with a rich variety of plants, let nature be your guide and replant this area with wildflowers.

The woodland floor is covered by a humusy material that resembles its origin, fallen leaves, more than it does garden soil. Every year, a nearly endlessly renewable resource of leaves falls to replenish the floor. For my own woodland garden, I outlined the area for the beds in logs and then filled in the space between the top edge of the logs and the base of the trees with organic material. I used whatever I could find that resembled the forest's somewhat acidic humus—composted sawdust, bits of decomposed fallen trees, composted horse manure, shredded bark mulch that had been aged for one year, and as much leaf mold (composted leaves) as possible. Every year, more autumn leaves enrich this imitation of the forest floor.

To find the plants discussed in this chapter, turn to native plant nurseries, plant society sales, and plant rescue groups. And don't forget seeds. You can buy seeds from many native plant societies.

Amsonia tabernaemontana
(blue dogbane)

Anemonella thalictroides
'Rosea Plena' ['Schoaff's
Double Pink'] (double
pink rue anemone)

Asarum spp.
(wild ginger)

RIGHT
Camassia scilloides
(wild hyacinth)

AMSONIA TABERNAEMONTANA

PRONUNCIATION: am-SONE-ee-a tab-er-nay-mon-TAN-a

COMMON NAME: Blue dogbane, bluestar, willow amsonia

HOMELAND: Riverbanks and damp woods of New Jersey to Tennessee, and south to Georgia and Texas

HARDINESS: USDA Zones 3–9

SIZE: 2'–4' tall; 2'–3' across

INTEREST: Branched clusters of pale blue starry flowers top strong stems in mid-spring. Amber fall foliage.

LIGHT CONDITIONS: Full sun to partial shade

SOIL/MOISTURE: Tolerates a wide range of soils, but should not dry out excessively

DESCRIPTION: Blue dogbane makes substantial clumps of erect stems, crowded with glossy, oblong leaves up to 6″ long. The ½″ flowers open from gray-blue buds, and are arranged in dome-shaped clusters. A suitable companion for turtleheads, closed gentians, and ferns in damp woodlands. As an ornamental, blue dogbane requires little maintenance and adapts well to partially shaded positions in the garden. Sear the base of the milky-sapped stems in a gas flame if used as a cut flower.

ANEMONELLA THALICTROIDES 'ROSEA PLENA'

PRONUNCIATION: an-em-on-ELL-a thal-ik-TROY-dees

COMMON NAME: Double pink rue anemone

HOMELAND: Of garden origin; species grows in woodland communities of the Northeast to Florida, Missouri, and Kansas

HARDINESS: USDA Zones 3–8

SIZE: 4″–8″ tall; 4″–6″ across

INTEREST: Double, deep pink to lavender-pink ½″ flowers, bloom in spring. Several cluster loosely above a ruff of pale green, 3-lobed leaves.

LIGHT CONDITIONS: Partial shade to shade

SOIL/MOISTURE: Highly organic woodland soil that does not dry out

DESCRIPTION: Double pink rue anemone is an especially charming ephemeral, well suited to accompany hepaticas, spring beauties, and ferns in woodland communities, or even in shaded rock gardens. The species has pristine white flowers and colonizes slowly. Both species and cultivars become dormant as the temperature rises in late spring.

ASARUM SPP.

PRONUNCIATION: a-SAIR-um

COMMON NAME: Wild ginger

HOMELAND: Dry or damp woodlands throughout much of the temperate regions of North America

HARDINESS: USDA Zones 4–9

SIZE: 6"–10" tall; 10"–12" across

INTEREST: Evergreen or deciduous heart-shaped leaves, often mottled or traced with silver. Almost hidden, triangular, brown 1"–2" flowers.

LIGHT CONDITIONS: Bright or partial shade to shade

SOIL/MOISTURE: Moist or dry soil of average fertility

DESCRIPTION: The several North American species include *A. canadense*, Canada wild ginger, which has deciduous, matte green leaves covered with down growing from thick rhizomes. It spreads slowly, and is found in eastern North America. *A. virginicum*, *A. shuttleworthii*, and *A. caudatum* are evergreen. The former two species have leaves that are blunted at the tip; their ranges overlap from Virginia and West Virginia to Alabama and Georgia. The western species, *A. caudatum*, has shiny, kidney-shaped leaves. All make excellent ground covers. The curious flowers, borne right on the ground, are pollinated by tiny flies.

CAMASSIA SCILLOIDES

PRONUNCIATION: kam-ASS-ee-a sil-OY-dees

COMMON NAME: Wild hyacinth, Eastern camass

HOMELAND: Open woodlands and meadows of the East and Midwest, south to Georgia, Alabama and Texas

HARDINESS: USDA Zones 3–9

SIZE: 1'–2' tall; 1'–2' across

INTEREST: In late spring, erect spikes of 1", pale blue, 6-pointed flowers rise from a tuft of keeled, grassy leaves

LIGHT CONDITIONS: Full sun to light shade

SOIL/MOISTURE: Moist, rich, well-drained soil

DESCRIPTION: Wild hyacinth grows from a bulb and colonizes slowly. There are also several western species which were once highly prized for food by Native American tribes. Wild hyacinth is underused as an ornamental, but is ideal for light woodland gardens, where it supplies a welcome vertical dimension to spring plantings. It is a suitable companion for Allegheny foamflower, Canada wild ginger, and shrubby fothergillas.

Chrysogonum virginianum
(green 'n' gold)

Dicentra eximia
(fringed bleeding heart)

Disporum maculatum
(nodding mandarin)

LEFT
Dodecatheon meadia
(common shooting star)

CHRYSOGONUM VIRGINIANUM

PRONUNCIATION: kris-OG-o-num
vir-jin-ee-AYE-num

COMMON NAME: Green 'n' gold, Virginia
goldenstar

HOMELAND: In moist, shaded woodlands of
southern Pennsylvania and Ohio south to
Florida and Louisiana

HARDINESS: USDA Zones 4–10

SIZE: 6″–15″ tall; 6″–12″ across

INTEREST: Star-shaped, golden yellow flowerheads bloom in spring above a mat or
mound of rich green paddle-shaped leaves

LIGHT CONDITIONS: Light shade to shade

SOIL/MOISTURE: Moist but well-drained soil,
enriched with organic matter

DESCRIPTION: Green 'n gold is a perky little ground cover, well suited to the edges of woodland areas or as an underplanting for rhododendrons or mountain laurels. It is somewhat variable in its natural habitat. In the garden the spring flush of bloom is followed by sporadic flowers during hot weather, and often a lighter flush occurs again when night temperatures drop in fall. It self-sows, and colonizes by above-ground runners, but seldom becomes a nuisance.

DICENTRA EXIMIA

PRONUNCIATION: dye-SEN-tra eks-EEM-ee-a

COMMON NAME: Fringed bleeding heart, wild
bleeding heart

HOMELAND: Rocky woodlands and ledges of
the Appalachian and Catskill mountains south
to Georgia and Tennessee

HARDINESS: USDA Zones 3–10

SIZE: 12″–18″ tall; 12″–18″ across

INTEREST: Arching racemes of deep pink
heart-shaped flowers in spring through fall,
above clumps of watery-stemmed, green or
bluish green ferny foliage

LIGHT CONDITIONS: Light or partial shade to
shade

SOIL/MOISTURE: Average to fertile, well-
drained soil, enriched with organic matter

DESCRIPTION: Fringed bleeding heart is a delicate-looking herbaceous perennial, which retains its foliage and continues to bloom through the season. Although the rhizomes do not colonize readily, the plant self-seeds freely. An excellent plant for shaded, rocky banks and woodlands, or transition areas between the formal garden and rough woods. Fringed bleeding heart has become popular as an ornamental; numerous hybrids and cultivars, with foliage variations of color and dissection, and flower color from white to deep purplish pink, are on the market. They are useful additions to perennial and mixed beds and borders.

DISPORUM MACULATUM

PRONUNCIATION: dis-POR-um
mak-eve-LAY-tum

COMMON NAME: Nodding mandarin

HOMELAND: Wooded areas of Ohio and
southern Michigan, south to Georgia and
Alabama

HARDINESS: USDA Zones 5–8

SIZE: 12″–24″ tall; 12″–18″ across

INTEREST: In spring, nodding 1″ creamy white
flowers speckled with purple top branched
stems. Hairy yellow berries follow

LIGHT CONDITIONS: Light shade

SOIL/MOISTURE: Moisture-retentive, humusy
soil

DESCRIPTION: Nodding mandarin is rare. Its habit is similar to that of the better known *Uvularia*; its stalkless 4″ oblong leaves are clothed with bristly hairs beneath. It colonizes slowly by rhizomes. Appropriate in woodland gardens with Virginia bluebells, ferns, creeping phlox, and other shade-loving natives.

DODECATHEON MEADIA

PRONUNCIATION: doe-de-KATH-ee-on
MEE-dee-a

COMMON NAME: Common shooting star,
American cowslip

HOMELAND: Meadow, prairie and open woods
communities of Pennsylvania to Wisconsin,
and south to Texas and Georgia

HARDINESS: USDA Zones 4–9

SIZE: 1′–2′ tall; 1′ across

INTEREST: In spring and early summer, strong
scapes bear umbels of white or pink dart-
shaped flowers above rosettes of paddle-
shaped leaves

LIGHT CONDITIONS: Partial shade to shade

SOIL/MOISTURE: Well-drained, woodland soil
enriched with organic matter

DESCRIPTION: The flowers of common shooting star are interesting for their unusual swept back petals, which reveal a sharply pointed beak of stamens. Spreads very slowly by seed. The plants are dormant in summer. Although it is sometimes difficult to grow under cultivated conditions, this underused perennial is a charming addition to woodland gardens and is an attractive companion for ferns, which later camouflage its dying foliage. The western species, such as Sierra shooting star (*D. jeffreyi*), are similar.

Jeffersonia diphylla
(twinleaf)

Mertensia virginica
(Virginia bluebells)

Osmunda regalis
(royal fern)

RIGHT
Phlox stolonifera
(creeping phlox)

JEFFERSONIA DIPHYLLA

PRONUNCIATION: jeff-er-SO-nee-a dye-FILL-a

COMMON NAME: Twinleaf, rheumatism-root

HOMELAND: Woodlands of Wisconsin, southern Ontario, and western New York, south to Georgia and Alabama

HARDINESS: USDA Zones 5–8

SIZE: 10″–18″ tall; 12″ across

INTEREST: Loose clumps of long-stemmed, gray-green leaves, deeply cleft into 2 kidney-shaped lobes. Solitary 1″ pure white flowers in early spring.

LIGHT CONDITIONS: Light-dappled shade

SOIL/MOISTURE: Moist woodland soil enriched with organic matter

DESCRIPTION: Twinleaf is charming for its early spring bloom, but really makes a show later as the foliage expands after the fruit capsule is ripe. The leaf blades may reach 6″ long and 5″ across. Most effective as a companion for ferns of all sorts. Named for President Thomas Jefferson, a noted patron of horticulture.

MERTENSIA VIRGINICA

PRONUNCIATION: mer-TEN-see-a vur-JIN-ik-a

COMMON NAME: Virginia bluebells, Virginia cowslip

HOMELAND: Damp woods, meadows, and streamsides from eastern Minnesota to Ontario and New York, south to South Carolina, Arkansas, and Kansas

HARDINESS: USDA Zones 3–9

SIZE: 1′–2′ tall; 1′–2′ across

INTEREST: In early spring, coiled clusters of pink buds open to nodding, sky-blue, 1″ trumpet-shaped flowers. The oval leaves may reach 4″ in length.

LIGHT CONDITIONS: Partial shade to shade

SOIL/MOISTURE: Moist, acid, woodsy soil, high in organic matter

DESCRIPTION: Virginia bluebells is one of our favorite wildflowers. The strongly veined leaves die back after the blooming season, when the plant goes dormant. Excellent in a light woodland setting. Plant with ostrich fern, cinnamon fern, or lady fern, which will hide the yellowing foliage; also good with fringed bleeding hearts for a pink and blue combination; and the perfect foil for white *Trillium grandiflorum.* The plants spread slowly, but in time will colonize an area. White-flowered forms sometimes appear in a population.

OSMUNDA REGALIS

PRONUNCIATION: oz-MUN-da re-GAL-is

COMMON NAME: Royal fern

HOMELAND: In swamps and shaded wetlands of eastern North America, Europe, and the tropical areas of the Americas

HARDINESS: USDA Zones 3–10

SIZE: 2'–5' tall; 3'–5' across

INTEREST: Upright clumps of pale green oblong fronds twice cut into widely spaced leaflets; terminal brown fertile leaflets

LIGHT CONDITIONS: Bright shade to shade

SOIL/MOISTURE: Wet, humusy, or muck soil, or shallow standing water

DESCRIPTION: Royal fern spreads slowly by rhizomes, and in suitable locations develops into extensive stands. Excellent beside ponds or slow-running streams in woodland settings. In gardens it will tolerate less moisture and is appropriate for planting among rhododendrons and other shade-loving shrubs in soil that is high in humus.

PHLOX STOLONIFERA

PRONUNCIATION: FLOX sto-lon-IF-era

COMMON NAME: Creeping phlox

HOMELAND: Moist woods and bottomlands of the Appalachian region, south to Georgia

HARDINESS: USDA Zones 3–9

SIZE: 6"–12" tall; 12"–15" across

INTEREST: Mats of evergreen foliage, with erect stems crowned with clusters of 2–3 pinkish purple, 1"–1½" flowers in spring

LIGHT CONDITIONS: Partial or dappled shade to shade; tolerates sun in cool zones

SOIL/MOISTURE: Moist, humus-rich soil

DESCRIPTION: A good companion for spring beauties, rue anemones, and trilliums, which often share the same community. Creeping phlox, perhaps the most shade tolerant of the phlox species, forms wide, stoloniferous mats of foliage. The stems and flowers are covered in fine hair; the petals are rarely notched. Popular as an ornamental ground cover plant for woodlands. Several cultivars are available, including 'Bruce's White' and 'Pink Ridge'.

Sanguinaria canadensis
(bloodroot)

Stylophorum diphyllum
(celandine poppy)

Tiarella cordifolia
(foamflower)

LEFT
Trillium grandiflorum
(large white trillium)

SANGUINARIA CANADENSIS

PRONUNCIATION: san-gwin-AIR-ee-a
can-a-DEN-sis

COMMON NAME: Bloodroot, red puccoon

HOMELAND: Rich or dry rocky woodland
slopes and along streams in open areas of
Quebec to Manitoba; south to Florida,
Alabama, and Oklahoma

HARDINESS: USDA Zones 3–9

SIZE: 6″–9″ tall; 12″–15″ across

INTEREST: In early spring, gray-green leaves
unfurl to reveal buds, which open into glis-
tening white 1½″ flowers

LIGHT CONDITIONS: Light-dappled shade to
shade

SOIL/MOISTURE: Average, acid to alkaline,
humusy soil

DESCRIPTION: Grown at Monticello by Thomas Jefferson, and cherished by generations of nature lovers, bloodroot blooms only fleetingly. However, its
durable, wavy, lobed foliage, which expands to 1′ across, remains until fall if
moisture is sufficient. The clumps of roots can be divided to propagate; broken
roots bleed a reddish sap, which Native Americans used as a body paint and dye
for clothing. Bloodroot has multiple medicinal uses, and extracts of it are added
to some toothpastes as an antiplaque agent. A double-flowered cultivar is available that has the same foliar attributes, but is showier in bloom.

STYLOPHORUM DIPHYLLUM

PRONUNCIATION: sty-low-FOR-um
dye-FILL-um

COMMON NAME: Celandine poppy, wood
poppy

HOMELAND: Rich, damp woods from
Pennsylvania and Wisconsin south to Georgia
and Arkansas

HARDINESS: USDA Zones 4–9

SIZE: 12″–18″ tall; 15″–24″ across

INTEREST: Bright yellow 1½″–2″ poppy flowers bloom from early spring to early summer,
each between a pair of pale green, deeply
lobed leaves

LIGHT CONDITIONS: Light-dappled shade to
shade

SOIL/MOISTURE: Moist, woodland soil

DESCRIPTION: Celandine poppy self-seeds freely from egg-shaped, hairy seedpods
and develops large colonies. If dead-headed, it will bloom whenever temperatures are cool, but the dangling fruits are almost as ornamental as the blossoms.
It is ideal for woodland communities and is a suitable companion for Virginia
bluebells, fringed bleeding hearts, and wild sweet William. The yellow sap was
used as a dye by Native Americans.

TIARELLA CORDIFOLIA

PRONUNCIATION: tee-are-ELL-a
cor-di-FOE-lee-a

COMMON NAME: Foamflower, Allegheny
foamflower

HOMELAND: Woodland communities from
Nova Scotia to Wisconsin, south to Georgia
and Mississippi

HARDINESS: USDA Zones 3–9

SIZE: 6″–12″ tall; 12″–15″ across

INTEREST: In spring, fluffy spikes of starry,
white ¼″ flowers bloom above clumps of
dark green, heart-shaped, lobed leaves

LIGHT CONDITIONS: Partial shade to shade

SOIL/MOISTURE: Moisture-retentive, organic
soil, enriched with humus

DESCRIPTION: Foamflower spreads by stolons and colonizes quite quickly, except in dry soils, which it tolerates. It makes an excellent ground cover and is a suitable companion for trilliums, creeping phlox, false Solomon's seal, and many other spring wildflowers and ferns. The leaves remain handsome throughout the season. Popular in ornamental gardens, especially since cultivars with foliage variations resembling oak or maple leaves have been introduced on the market, as well as long-blooming and pink-tinged selections.

TRILLIUM GRANDIFLORUM

PRONUNCIATION: TRIL-lee-um
grand-i-FLOR-um

COMMON NAME: Large white trillium, wake
robin, snow trillium

HOMELAND: Thickets and rich woodland communities from Quebec to Minnesota, south to
Pennsylvania and Arkansas

HARDINESS: USDA Zones 3–9

SIZE: 12″–18″ tall; 12″–15″ across

INTEREST: In spring, 3-petaled, pure white
2″–4″ flowers open 3″ or so above the
leaves, which are divided into 3 broad
leaflets

LIGHT CONDITIONS: Partial or dappled shade

SOIL/MOISTURE: Deep, rich, moisture-
retentive soil

DESCRIPTION: Trilliums are perhaps among the most cherished of our native flora. A stand of them beneath deciduous trees is a sight to remember. The flowers of this variable species age to pink; the plants become dormant after the blooming. A good companion for spring beauties and ferns. Long cultivated in gardens, they are slow to reproduce, and have been collected illegally from the wild to satisfy the demands in this country and overseas. 'Quicksilver' reproduces more quickly; it shows promise in the marketplace. Double-flowered forms are available, but are rare. Wild plants must not be dug up.

Uvularia grandiflora
(wood merry-bells)

Veratrum viride
(Indian poke)

Xanthorhiza simplicissima
(yellowroot)

RIGHT
Viola labradorica
(Labrador violet)

UVULARIA GRANDIFLORA

PRONUNCIATION: ewe-vew-LARE-ee-a grand-i-FLOR-a

COMMON NAME: Wood merry-bells, large-flowered bellwort, great merry-bells

HOMELAND: Rich woodlands from Quebec to the Dakotas and south to Georgia and Oklahoma

HARDINESS: USDA Zones 3–9

SIZE: 12"–30" tall; 12"–24" across

INTEREST: Yellow, twisted, bell-shaped 2" flowers hang from branched stems, above clasping, drooping leaves

LIGHT CONDITIONS: Light shade; full sun in cool climates

SOIL/MOISTURE: Moist, alkaline soil, high in organic matter

DESCRIPTION: Wood merry-bells is a good companion in woodlands for later-emerging ferns, but is also attractive combined with different species of trilliums, Jacob's ladder, and creeping phlox. After blooming season, the foliage straightens and is more attractive. Established plants are bold enough to highlight a rock ledge. Provide a summer mulch to maintain the soil moisture level.

VERATRUM VIRIDE

PRONUNCIATION: ver-AY-trum VEE-ri-dee

COMMON NAME: Indian poke, false hellebore

HOMELAND: Wet woods and swamps of southern Canada and the northern United States, south to Georgia

HARDINESS: USDA Zones 3–7

SIZE: 3'–6' tall; 2' or more across

INTEREST: Bold, pleated leaves to 1' long; in summer, tall branched spikes crowded with yellow-green, star-shaped 1" flowers

LIGHT CONDITIONS: Part sun to light shade

SOIL/MOISTURE: Moist, even wet, soil enriched with humus

DESCRIPTION: An imposing plant for wet areas, Indian poke is commonly found growing in the wild in wet woodland communities above skunk cabbages with turtleheads and lobelias, among rushes and tussock sedges. It does best where heat and humidity are not excessive; if it dries out, the leaf margins become desiccated and brown. The stems are clothed with leaves to the base of the hairy flower spikes, which may reach 18"–24" in length; the lower branches droop. In spite of all parts of this plant being highly poisonous, it has been used medicinally for hundreds of years, particularly to lower blood pressure.

VIOLA LABRADORICA

PRONUNCIATION: vi-OH-la lab-ra-DOR-ik-a
COMMON NAME: Labrador violet
HOMELAND: Poor, gravelly, and sandy soils from Greenland and Newfoundland to Alaska, and south to New Hampshire and Minnesota
HARDINESS: USDA Zones 3–8
SIZE: 1″–6″ tall; 3″–4″ across

INTEREST: In spring, deep purple flowers bloom among tufts of 1″ hairless, purple-tinted oval leaves, edged with rounded teeth
LIGHT CONDITIONS: Part shade to shade
SOIL/MOISTURE: Average well-drained or sandy soil, enriched with humus

DESCRIPTION: This low-growing violet colonizes slowly both by seed and by slender creeping rhizomes that lengthen after flowering time. An attractive woodland companion for creeping phlox and spring beauties, Labrador violets also make an interesting carpet beneath viburnums, dogwoods, Carolina silver bells, and other deciduous shrubs, and they are lovely planted beside woodland rock outcroppings.

XANTHORHIZA SIMPLICISSIMA

PRONUNCIATION: zan-tho-RI-za sim-pliss-ISS-im-a
COMMON NAME: Yellowroot
HOMELAND: Damp woodland areas from New York south to Florida
HARDINESS: USDA Zones 5–9
SIZE: 2′–3′ tall; 2′–3′ across

INTEREST: Delicate clusters of purplish flowers in spring, before the handsome, pinnate leaves appear. Rich bronze and purple fall color.
LIGHT CONDITIONS: Full sun or partial shade
SOIL/MOISTURE: Moisture-retentive, average soil, but tolerant of heavy clay soils

DESCRIPTION: Yellowroot is a deciduous shrub that spreads quickly by suckers to form dense mounds. It should only be planted where it can be confined or has plenty of room. It is excellent on banks beside streams, where the soil does not dry out. As a ground cover, it helps to control erosion. An easy, low-maintenance shrub, yellowroot provides good cover for wildlife.

Plants for the Water's Edge

Plants for the Water's Edge

Anyone who has water in his or her garden knows that this element brings life. Anyone who does not have a pond, brook, pool, birdbath, or even a trickling fountain should work toward creating some of this magic. In natural habitat gardens, we strive to develop what might already lie hidden in the landscape, perhaps in a moist spot beneath the alien "weeds," such as privet, multiflora rose, or Japanese honeysuckle. Another particularly appealing thing about the water's edge is that it supports the most unusual—some might even call them odd—plants in the garden.

One of my favorite plants of the water's edge is the lowly skunk cabbage (*Symplocarpus foetidus*). Broad leaves give the plant half its common name—it resembles a giant cabbage head—but if bruised, the first part of its name is clear: the leaves smell...bad. But if this malodor is overlooked (or violent confrontation is scrupulously avoided), skunk cabbage could be America's answer to the hosta. In winter the skunk cabbage's mahogany-colored twisted cones flecked with ocher push up through the snow like a troupe of diminutive monks. The snow melts in the space around the flowers, part of its secret stratagem for pollination. (The temperature inside the spathe is higher than the outside air, and insects are lured in for warmth, where in return for cozy shelter they pollinate their host.) In spring the spectacular leaves make their entrance.

Unfortunately, to my knowledge, not a single nursery sells this common plant (whenever I lament that fact in a lecture, members of the audience inevitably offer me as many as I would like). Difficult to transport, skunk cabbage is best propagated by collecting the ripe berrylike fruits in the early autumn. Don't wild-collect them, however tempting, for although the plants are far from endangered, their habitats are.

Water-loving plants are different, unique, and often rare, yet when I visit bogs and damp woodlands, though I am the stranger, the plants make me feel welcome. Precisely because they might find a home only in their natural habitats, they are all the more to be preserved and cherished.

Caltha palustris
'Flore Plena' (double
marsh marigold)

Chelone lyonii
(pink turtlehead)

Clethra alnifolia 'Rosea'
(pink summersweet)

RIGHT
Cephalanthus occidentalis
(buttonbush)

CALTHA PALUSTRIS 'FLORE PLENA'

PRONUNCIATION: KAL-tha pal-US-triss

COMMON NAME: Double marsh marigold, kingcup, cowslip

HOMELAND: Of garden origin; species found at shaded pond sides and riverbanks from Newfoundland to Alaska, south to North Carolina and Tennessee

HARDINESS: USDA Zones 3–9

SIZE: 1'–2' tall; 1'–1.5' across

INTEREST: Large, golden, buttercup flowers bloom in spring over heart-shaped, glossy foliage

LIGHT CONDITIONS: Partial shade to shade

SOIL/MOISTURE: Average soil that remains constantly moist

DESCRIPTION: This harbinger of spring becomes dormant when temperatures rise. The species may be found growing in the wild with royal ferns and later-blooming great blue lobelia and turtleheads, often under high, deciduous shade. The same combination, using the double-flowered cultivar, works well in ornamental gardens, in bog gardens, or beside streams. Provides good cover for frogs and turtles.

CEPHALANTHUS OCCIDENTALIS

PRONUNCIATION: sef-al-AN-thus ox-id-en-TAHL-is

COMMON NAME: Buttonbush

HOMELAND: Standing water and wet sites from Nova Scotia to Florida, and west to Minnesota and California

HARDINESS: USDA Zones 5–10

SIZE: 3'–12' tall; 4'–10' across

INTEREST: In mid- in to late summer, fragrant, tiny white flowers crowd into dense, 1" spherical heads on dense, leafy shrubs

LIGHT CONDITIONS: Full sun to partial shade

SOIL/MOISTURE: Very wet, neutral to acid soils, or in standing water

DESCRIPTION: Buttonbush is good to naturalize in the landscape, where it can spread and develop into thickets, but it also makes a handsome specimen in a wet spot. The glossy foliage is attractive in summer; in fall it turns dull yellow. The espresso-brown seed balls persist for several months. A superior wildlife plant, it is a preferred nectar source for ruby-throated hummingbirds, and the seeds provide food for several species of waterfowl. Red-winged blackbirds use it for cover and nesting sites.

CHELONE LYONII

PRONUNCIATION: key-LONE-ee LION-ee-i

COMMON NAME: Pink turtlehead

HOMELAND: Bogs and streamsides of the Appalachian regions to the Carolinas and Tennessee

HARDINESS: USDA Zones 4–9

SIZE: 1.5'–3.5' tall; 2'–3' across

INTEREST: Clusters of 2"-long, rosy pink flowers bloom in late summer above clumps of erect stems that are well clothed with dark green, toothed leaves

LIGHT CONDITIONS: Light, dappled shade or light shade

SOIL/MOISTURE: Average fertility, moist or even boggy soil

DESCRIPTION: Pink turtlehead is often found growing in swamps with great blue lobelia and cardinal flower, as well as with royal and other ferns. It tolerates sunny locations if they remain damp; stress caused by drought encourages attack from mildew. A larval food plant for Baltimore checkerspots; a nectar plant for numerous butterflies.

CLETHRA ALNIFOLIA 'ROSEA'

PRONUNCIATION: KLETH-ra all-ni-FO-lee-a

COMMON NAME: Pink summersweet, pink sweet pepperbush

HOMELAND: Of garden origin; the white-flowered species is found in sandy, swampy areas from Maine to Florida

HARDINESS: USDA Zones 4–9

SIZE: 3'–6' tall; 3'–6' across

INTEREST: In late summer, 2"–6" spikes of pink, fragrant flowers bloom atop a dense, leafy, round-topped shrub

LIGHT CONDITIONS: Light shade; full sun if there is sufficient moisture

SOIL/MOISTURE: Moist acid, soil, high in organic matter

DESCRIPTION: Summersweet is an understory shrub that grows in wet areas and colonizes by stolons. At bloom time, its spicy fragrance is unforgettable and the shrubs are alive with butterflies and insects gathering nectar and pollen. Its dense bushy growth provides good cover for birds. Valuable massed in wet areas or planted as a hedge. 'Rosea' has all the attributes of the species and has attractive pink flower buds which open to soft pink, and then mature to pinkish white flowers. All are particularly striking in fall when the foliage turns bright yellow. 'Hummingbird' is an excellent 4' cultivar with white flowers.

Gentiana andrewsii
(bottle gentian)

Helonias bullata
(swamp pink)

Iris versicolor
(blue flag iris)

LEFT
Hibiscus moscheutos
(swamp rose mallow)

GENTIANA ANDREWSII

PRONUNCIATION: jen-SHEE-an-a
an-DREWS-ee-i

COMMON NAME: Bottle gentian, closed gentian

HOMELAND: Bogs, meadows, and wet areas throughout eastern North America

HARDINESS: USDA Zones 3–7

SIZE: 12″–24″ tall; 12″–18″ across

INTEREST: In late summer and fall, clusters of pure, deep blue, flask-shaped flowers that never open are borne on unbranched stems in the upper leaf axils

LIGHT CONDITIONS: Sun to light shade

SOIL/MOISTURE: Moist, acid soil of average fertility, enriched with organic matter

---

DESCRIPTION: Bottle gentian combines well with moisture-loving grasses and ferns, and is a useful companion for cardinal flowers, which bloom at about the same time. Tolerant of sunny sites if moisture is sufficient, or if shaded from the noonday sun. Pollinators crawl inside the budlike flowers and dance about before exiting covered with pollen.

HELONIAS BULLATA

PRONUNCIATION: hell-OWN-ee-as bul-AH-ta

COMMON NAME: Swamp pink

HOMELAND: Swamps and boggy areas along the coasts of New York and New Jersey to Virginia and North Carolina

HARDINESS: USDA Zones 4–8

SIZE: 15″–18″ tall; 6″–8″ across

INTEREST: In spring, a sturdy stem topped with an egg-shaped cluster of starry, bright pink, ¼″ flowers rises from a basal rosette of evergreen, lance-shaped leaves

LIGHT CONDITIONS: Light shade, or sun if moisture is adequate

SOIL/MOISTURE: Moisture-retentive, well-drained, acid soil, enriched with humus

---

DESCRIPTION: An interesting and underused plant for bog gardens and other wet sites, swamp pink deserves a wider audience. Its clusters of fragrant flowers are showy and bloom at the same time as marsh marigolds and skunk cabbage, which flourish in the same habitat.

HIBISCUS MOSCHEUTOS

PRONUNCIATION: hi-BIS-cus mos-CHEW-tus

COMMON NAME: Swamp rose mallow

HOMELAND: Saltwater and freshwater marshes of Massachusetts to Michigan and south to Alabama and Georgia

HARDINESS: USDA Zones 5–9

SIZE: 5'–7' tall; 3'–5' across

INTEREST: Bold shrublike plants with large heart-shaped, toothed leaves; huge pink or red flowers bloom from mid-summer to fall

LIGHT CONDITIONS: Sun to light shade

SOIL/MOISTURE: Rich soil that does not dry out in summer

DESCRIPTION: This statuesque perennial is well-suited to streamside or pond side gardens where it can be somewhat protected from strong winds by other vegetation. In its native habitat it often grows with water-loving shrubs, tall grasses, rushes, and cattails. The showy, giant-single-hollyhocklike flowers can reach 8" across and often have a central crimson eye. Overblown "dinner plate" strains such as Disco Belle are to be avoided in natural gardens. Interesting dry fruits provide post-frost interest.

IRIS VERSICOLOR

PRONUNCIATION: EYE-ris VERS-i-co-lor

COMMON NAME: Blue flag iris, wild iris

HOMELAND: Marshes and wet meadows of eastern Canada and Maine, east to Minnesota, and south to Virginia

HARDINESS: USDA Zones 3–9

SIZE: 1'–3' tall; 1'–2' across

INTEREST: In late spring and early summer, branched stems carry several lavender or violet 2"–3" flowers. Attractive clumps of wide, sword-shaped leaves.

LIGHT CONDITIONS: Full sun to light shade

SOIL/MOISTURE: Humus-enriched moist soil

DESCRIPTION: Blue flag iris is an indispensable plant in damp meadow or streamside communities, sharing its habitat with cattails, pitcher plants, and marsh marigolds. It is also suitable for the edges of informal ponds or in streamside gardens. The arching leaves remain handsome through the summer, provided there is sufficient moisture available. It is a strong grower and helps to control bank erosion. The tubers are a favorite food of muskrats.

Lobelia siphilitica
(great blue lobelia)

Orontium aquaticum
(golden club)

Lysichiton americanum
(western skunk cabbage)

RIGHT
Nymphaea odorata
(fragrant water lily)

LOBELIA SIPHILITICA

PRONUNCIATION: low-BEE-lee-a sif-ill-IT-ik-a

COMMON NAME: Great blue lobelia, blue lobelia

HOMELAND: Pond, streamsides, wet meadows, and marshes from Manitoba to western New England, and south to Alabama and Texas

HARDINESS: USDA Zones 4–9

SIZE: 2′–5′ tall; 2′–3′ across

INTEREST: Substantial clumps of sturdy spikes of blue or purplish flowers in late summer and fall

LIGHT CONDITIONS: Full sun to shade

SOIL/MOISTURE: Fertile or average soils that remain moist are best, although it will tolerate drier conditions

DESCRIPTION: Great blue lobelia has basal rosettes of toothed, lance-shaped leaves, with flower spikes that bloom well above the mass of foliage. Each 2-lipped flower is about 1″ long. The blue upper lip splits into 2 teeth; the 3-lobed lower lip and the belly of the flowers are striped with white. Populations sometimes include white-flowered forms. Great blue lobelia is found growing in swampy areas with other wet-soil lovers such as turtleheads, rushes, and sedges. The strong roots penetrate deeply into the soil, providing stability and anchorage for other plants to colonize.

LYSICHITON AMERICANUM

PRONUNCIATION: lis-i-KITE-on am-er-ik-AIN-um

COMMON NAME: Western skunk cabbage, yellow skunk cabbage

HOMELAND: Swamps and wetlands of California to Alaska, east to Idaho and Montana

HARDINESS: USDA Zones 6–9

SIZE: 2′–4′ tall; 2′–3′ across

INTEREST: In mid-spring, before the huge leaves develop, a 6″–7″ yellow hood (spathe) appears around a stout stem (spadix), which bears minute buff flowers

LIGHT CONDITIONS: Full sun to part shade

SOIL/MOISTURE: Deep wet or damp soils enriched with humus

DESCRIPTION: The waxy spathes of Western skunk cabbage are very showy in the spring landscape and attract pollinating insects to the minute flowers that appear on the 6″ spadix. The elliptical leaves, 3′ to 5′ long, release a strong skunk-like odor when bruised, so avoid planting next to waterside seating areas. By midsummer the plants are dormant. The thick rhizomes provide food for aquatic mammals and other wildlife. Best propagated from fresh seed. Rare in the trade.

Nymphaea odorata

PRONUNCIATION: nim-FAY-a-o-dor-AH-ta

COMMON NAME: Fragrant water lily, white water lily

HOMELAND: Ponds and lakes from Newfoundland to Manitoba, also Michigan, Florida, and Louisiana

HARDINESS: USDA Zones 3–10

SIZE: Floating, 4'–7' across

INTEREST: Many-petaled, white, fragrant flowers bloom from early summer through fall, above almost circular leaves

LIGHT CONDITIONS: Full sun

SOIL/MOISTURE: Rich clay soil beneath 8"–18" of standing water

DESCRIPTION: The starry 2"–4" flowers often extend a few inches out of the water. They open during the day and close at night, and they remain closed on very cloudy days. The smooth, glossy, dark green leaves are 4"–9" across; they are maroon or purplish on the underside. Fragrant water lily colonizes slowly and provides cover and food for frogs, turtles, aquatic mammals, and fish. The seeds also provide food for wildlife. Pink forms sometimes appear, and there are numerous hybrids and cultivars available in many flower colors, for garden use.

Orontium aquaticum

PRONUNCIATION: or-ON-tee-um ak-WAT-ik-um

COMMON NAME: Golden club

HOMELAND: Bogs and streamsides of the coastal plains from southern New York and Massachusetts to Florida and Mississippi

HARDINESS: USDA Zones 6–9

SIZE: Floating, 1'–2' across

INTEREST: In spring, a white pokerlike spadix tipped with 2"–4" of tiny, bright yellow flowers; elliptical blue-green 1' leaves follow

LIGHT CONDITIONS: Full sun

SOIL/MOISTURE: Acid, rich soil beneath 6"–12" of water

DESCRIPTION: Golden club spreads freely and is appropriate for the edges of ponds, lakes, and slow-running streams, where the rhizomes help to control erosion. The long-stalked, waxy, parallel-veined leaves may reach 1', and are silvery on the underside. In shallow water they reach out beyond the surface, but they float where the water is deeper. Blue-green berries develop on the spadix after the flowers are fertilized. Golden club provides food and cover for aquatic mammals, turtles, frogs, and fish.

Sagittaria latifolia
(arrowhead)

Symplocarpus foetidus
(skunk cabbage)

Thalia dealbata
(hardy water canna)

LEFT
Sarracenia purpurea
(northern pitcher plant)

SAGITTARIA LATIFOLIA

PRONUNCIATION: saj-it-AIR-ee-a
lat-i-FO-lee-a

COMMON NAME: Arrowhead, duck potato

HOMELAND: Mud and wet, sandy swamps
from Nova Scotia to British Columbia and
south to Florida and Mexico

HARDINESS: USDA Zones 4–9

SIZE: 1′–3′ tall; 1′–2′ across

INTEREST: Dramatic arrow-shaped leaves,
among which spikes of showy white 3-parted
flowers bloom in mid-summer to fall

LIGHT CONDITIONS: Full sun to light shade

SOIL/MOISTURE: Moist, sandy soil, or standing water

DESCRIPTION: The foliage shape of arrowhead is quite variable, ranging from slender and narrow to broadly triangular. A great addition to waterside garden settings; tolerant of confinement in a container for small pools. The large tubers were a valuable starchy food source for Native Americans and are stored by muskrats for winter provisions. The handsome white flowers peek out above the foliage and last a long time. This is one of the showier waterside natives.

SARRACENIA PURPUREA

PRONUNCIATION: sar-a-SEEN-ee-a
pur-PEWR-ee-a

COMMON NAME: Northern pitcher plant

HOMELAND: Sphagnum and peat bogs from
Minnesota to New Jersey and south along the
coast to Florida

HARDINESS: USDA Zones 4–9

SIZE: 12″–24″ tall; 12″–18″ across

INTEREST: Clumps of evergreen, purple-tinged,
4″–6″ long inflated leaves (pitchers) give rise
to leafless stems that end in rich maroon
nodding flowers in spring

LIGHT CONDITIONS: Full sun

SOIL/MOISTURE: Moist, well-drained, sandy,
acid soil

DESCRIPTION: Northern pitcher plants are often considered little more than curiosities, but they are an essential component of sphagnum bogs, especially in the north, and they adapt well to sandy, acid bog gardens. The curved pitchers often fill halfway with water. Small insects, attracted to the open lip, or mouth, of the pitchers, slide down the coarse, downward-pointing hairs within, drown, and then are digested by plant enzymes. The fascinating 2″ flowers are globular; the central umbrella-shaped style, which covers the 5 stigmas, persists for several weeks. There are several localized subspecies.

SYMPLOCARPUS FOETIDUS

PRONUNCIATION: sim-plo-CAR-pus FET-id-us

COMMON NAME: Skunk cabbage

HOMELAND: Wet soil in woods, swamps, and along streams in southern Canada and the northern United States

HARDINESS: USDA Zones 2–7

SIZE: 1'–3' tall; 2'–4' across

INTEREST: In late winter, a shell-like, maroon hood (spathe), mottled with ocher and green, envelops a rounded stem (spadix); fresh green leaves develop later

LIGHT CONDITIONS: Light to medium shade

SOIL/MOISTURE: Moisture-retentive, fertile soil, muck, or clay

DESCRIPTION: Skunk cabbage colonizes areas along streams and riverbanks. Often found growing in the wild with royal ferns and marsh marigolds. The curious 2"–6" inflorescences are sometimes visible as early as Thanksgiving, but they are sure to have pushed through the frozen ground, and even snow, by New Year's Day. The spadix bears minute perfect flowers, which are pollinated by tiny flies, and elongates to 3"–6" when in fruit. The broad, oval 18" leaves expand later, on 12" petioles; both have a strong odor when bruised. Closely related to Western skunk cabbage, *Lysichiton americanum.*

THALIA DEALBATA

PRONUNCIATION: TH-ay-lee-a deel-BAY-ta

COMMON NAME: Hardy water canna, powdery thalia

HOMELAND: Swampy woodlands along the coastal plains from Florida to Texas, and inland from South Carolina to Missouri

HARDINESS: USDA Zones 7–9

SIZE: 4'–8' tall; 1'–3' across

INTEREST: Tropical-looking foliage, covered in a white powder; in summer, wands of purple flower spikes bloom above the leaves

LIGHT CONDITIONS: Full sun to light shade

SOIL/MOISTURE: Moist fertile soil or muck under 1'–2' of water

DESCRIPTION: The elliptical 12"–18" long leaves, covered with powdery meal, are carried on long petioles. Spikes of purple-violet flowers bloom on branched panicles well above the foliage. An unusual plant for bog gardens, ponds, or streamsides. In cold areas, plant in a container and protect during the winter. Mulch well if grown outdoors, unless covered by 1'–2' of water.

Berries,
Pods, and
Seeds for
Ornament
and Wildlife

Berries, Pods, and Seeds for Ornament and Wildlife

"Wildlife value" is the phrase that environmental gardeners use to describe a plant's impact on the animals that live in its area, but it means far more than just berries for the birds. There are plants that provide shelter, for instance, such as the eastern red cedar (*Juniperus virginiana*), whose dense twigs and evergreen needles make excellent nesting sites—safe from predators and harsh winds. Attractive native species may also be sources of nectar for bees and butterflies; seeds, nuts, and fruits besides berries fortify birds and other warm-blooded animals. Since these symbiotic relationships are usually specific to particular plants, birds, and animals, it is important for us to plant indigenous fruiting plants whenever we can. When Margaret Roach, my coauthor for *The Natural Habitat Garden*, replaced exotic berry-bearing plants on her property with native ones, birds appeared that had not been seen in her community for generations.

Of course, we want our gardens to be beautiful as well as useful to us and the other inhabitants of our landscapes. We welcome the wonderful fruits of the *Actaea* spp., such as doll's eyes—white berries, each with a single black spot. Goldenseal (*Hydrastis canadensis*) leaves look like umbrellas with strawberries on top. *Halesia*, silverbell, is noted here for its winged brown fruits in the autumn; but in the spring, thousands of nodding white bell-like flowers bloom all over the branches, and then sprinkle the ground below like snow.

Oaks have the highest wildlife value of almost any plant —certainly number one among the trees. Birds nest in them, but it is of course the acorns that are the oaks' great gift. Every plant is important, but trees even have value after death, presenting housing opportunities. Fallen trees shelter small mammals that inhabit the forest floor, while standing dead trees, called snags, provide homes for birds. If there is a dead tree on your property that doesn't pose a threat to buildings or people, leave it standing until it falls. Even after its structure has completely collapsed, millions of microorganisms, and insects will still find food and shelter there. Ultimately, the tree decomposes to contribute organic material to the soil. In nature nothing is wasted.

Aesculus californica
(California buckeye)

Ceanothus 'Dark Star'
(wild lilac)

Cornus racemosus
(gray dogwood)

RIGHT
Callicarpa americana
(American beautyberry)

AESCULUS CALIFORNICA

PRONUNCIATION: ES-kul-us kal-i-FOR-ni-ka

COMMON NAME: California buckeye

HOMELAND: Dry hillsides and canyons in coastal ranges and in the foothills of the Sierra Nevada

HARDINESS: USDA Zones 7–9

SIZE: 10′–20′ tall; 10′ or more across

INTEREST: A spreading shrub or multistemmed small tree, with dark green palmately compound leaves; 4″–8″ long panicles of white or pink flowers in spring.

LIGHT CONDITIONS: Full sun

SOIL/MOISTURE: Dry soil of average fertility

DESCRIPTION: Although the leaves fall by late summer unless moisture is ample, the smooth silvery-gray bark and interesting silhouette make California buckeye a good all-season plant. In bloom it is spectacular, with large candelabras of fragrant flowers. The large, shiny cinnamon-colored seeds that follow are enclosed by a smooth green covering. Seldom cultivated outside its natural range.

CALLICARPA AMERICANA

PRONUNCIATION: kal-i-KAR-pa amer-ik-AY-na

COMMON NAME: American beautyberry, French mulberry

HOMELAND: Southern Maryland to North Carolina and Arkansas, south to Mexico and the West Indies

HARDINESS: USDA Zones 7–11

SIZE: 3′–8′ tall; 4′–8′ across

INTEREST: In early summer, dense clusters of pale lavender flowers are borne in the leaf axils. Violet ¼″ fruits follow in fall

LIGHT CONDITIONS: Full sun to light, high shade

SOIL/MOISTURE: Average, well-drained but moist acid to alkaline soil

DESCRIPTION: This unusual shrub is best massed, so the full effect of its brilliant purple fruit stands out. Provides cover for small mammals and birds. Birds such as the northern bobwhite seek the fruits in winter. A white-fruited form, 'Lactea', is also available. Although Asian beautyberries are more popular in the trade, the fruits of the American species are larger and showier by far.

Ceanothus 'Dark Star'

PRONUNCIATION: see-an-OH-thus
COMMON NAME: Dark Star wild lilac
HOMELAND: Of garden origin
HARDINESS: USDA Zones 8–10
SIZE: 5'–6' tall; 8'–10' across
INTEREST: In late spring and summer, the mass of small evergreen foliage is covered with 1½" clusters of very deep cobalt blue flowers
LIGHT CONDITIONS: Full sun
SOIL/MOISTURE: Well-drained, even dry soil of average fertility

DESCRIPTION: Dark Star is among the best of the many cultivars. The flowers are followed by numerous tiny red berries. These shrubs are not very long lived but are easy to propagate from summer cuttings. Tolerates coastal conditions, wind, and drought. Plant in large masses to provide cover and food for wildlife. Dark Star is not browsed by deer.

Cornus racemosus

PRONUNCIATION: KOR-nus ray-see-MO-sus
COMMON NAME: Gray dogwood
HOMELAND: Borders fields and forests, in thickets and hedgerows from Maine to Minnesota, and south to North Carolina and Oklahoma
HARDINESS: USDA Zones 4–8
SIZE: 10'–15' tall; and as wide
INTEREST: Multistemmed, gray-barked shrub with panicles of white flowers in spring; white fruits on red pedicels follow
LIGHT CONDITIONS: Sun to partial shade
SOIL/MOISTURE: Very adaptable, but moist, well-drained soil is ideal

DESCRIPTION: Gray dogwood, which forms long colonies in the wild, is a favorite of many species of birds. Its berries are popular with wild turkeys, common flickers, downy woodpeckers, and cardinals; gray catbirds use gray dogwood for food, cover, and nesting sites. In the garden it is valued for its fall and winter interest more than for its short bloom time. Group or mass in the landscape; especially useful for its tolerance of poor soil conditions. In the fall, leaves turn burgundy red.

Ferocactus spp.
(barrel cactus)

Gaultheria procumbens
(wintergreen)

Hydrastis canadensis
(goldenseal)

LEFT
Halesia spp.
(silverbell tree)

FEROCACTUS SPP.

PRONUNCIATION: FERR-o-cak-tus

COMMON NAME: Barrel cactus

HOMELAND: Desert and rocky grassland regions of southwestern U.S. and Mexico

HARDINESS: USDA Zones 9–11

SIZE: 1′–12′ tall; 1′–2′ across

INTEREST: Bold, architectural stems shaped like barrels, columns, cushions, or flat disks, covered with often colorful hooklike, bent, or twisted spines

LIGHT CONDITIONS: Full sun

SOIL/MOISTURE: Very free-draining, sandy loam

DESCRIPTION: The desert flora of the Southwest typically includes several species of barrel cactus growing with mostly annual wildflowers, grasses, and low shrubs. Where their natural ranges overlap, barrel cactus hybridize freely. Only large plants bloom, with bright orange, yellow, or red bowl-shaped flowers clustered at the top in summer, and followed by colorful fruits in fall. Excellent for desert gardens and for containers. They must be allowed to rest dry during the winter to avoid rotting. Barrel cactus have long been used by Native Americans for numerous purposes; they are also used by birds and small mammals for perching, nesting sites, and food.

GAULTHERIA PROCUMBENS

PRONUNCIATION: gall-THAIR-ee-a pro-CUM-bens

COMMON NAME: Wintergreen, checkerberry

HOMELAND: In acid woodlands and clearings from Newfoundland to Manitoba and south to Georgia, Alabama, and Michigan

HARDINESS: USDA Zones 3–8

SIZE: 4″–6″ tall; 12″–24″ across

INTEREST: In summer, ¼″ urn-shaped, white flowers bloom above mounds of shrubby, creeping stems, clad with 2″ oval leaves. Scarlet berries.

LIGHT CONDITIONS: Shade, but in cool areas adapts to full sun

SOIL/MOISTURE: Moist, strongly acid soil, enriched with humus

DESCRIPTION: The glossy evergreen foliage, which turns purplish in cold weather, has been a source of oil of wintergreen. The foliage and the fruit are strongly aromatic. Bears and some small mammals eat the berries, but many last through the winter. Often found with trailing arbutus and blueberries. Effective massed under high-pruned trees or in the open, and as a ground cover beneath mountain laurel, rhododendrons, and other acid-loving shrubs.

HALESIA SPP.

PRONUNCIATION: hal-EES-ee-a
COMMON NAME: Silverbell tree, snowdrop tree
HOMELAND: Woodlands and streamsides from West Virginia to Florida, Texas and eastern Oklahoma
HARDINESS: USDA Zones 4–8
SIZE: 30'–40' or more tall; 20'–30' across

INTEREST: Low-branched trees or multi-stemmed shrubs with clusters of bell-shaped white or blush pink flowers in spring
LIGHT CONDITIONS: Sun to light shade
SOIL/MOISTURE: Rich, moist, acid soil, high in organic matter

DESCRIPTION: The several species of silverbell tree are not as widely grown as they deserve. The flowers usually appear before the foliage, which turns yellow in fall and tends to drop earlier than most shrubs; dry, winged fruits follow and are decorative. A valuable understory woody plant in groups or as a specimen in damp woodland areas and on the edge of woods. A good companion for slightly earlier-blooming eastern redbuds and flowering dogwoods. *H. monticola* is the tallest; *H. diptera* is the shortest and is the last to bloom.

HYDRASTIS CANADENSIS

PRONUNCIATION: hi-DRAS-tiss can-a-DEN-sis
COMMON NAME: Goldenseal, yellow puccoon
HOMELAND: Rich woods and damp meadows from Vermont to Nebraska, south to Georgia and Arkansas
HARDINESS: USDA Zones 3–8
SIZE: 8"–24" tall; 8"–12" across

INTEREST: Broadly lobed, downy leaves, often puckered, with creamy white flowers in spring, followed by rounded clusters of deep pink fruit
LIGHT CONDITIONS: Light shade to shade
SOIL/MOISTURE: Moist acid to neutral soil, enriched with humus

DESCRIPTION: Because its thick yellow roots have been used extensively in herbal medicine for a variety of complaints, goldenseal has been overcollected in the wild. Large doses can be toxic. Originally used by Native Americans medicinally and as a dye plant. A good companion for ferns, trilliums, and spring beauties in moist shade under deciduous trees.

Ilex verticillata
(winterberry)

Opuntia spp.
(prickly pear)

Rubus odoratus
(thimbleberry)

RIGHT
Rhus typhina 'Laciniata'
(cutleaf staghorn sumac)

ILEX VERTICILLATA

PRONUNCIATION: EYE-lex ver-tiss-ill-AH-ta
COMMON NAME: Winterberry
HOMELAND: Swamps and wet areas in deciduous woodlands from Nova Scotia west to Wisconsin and south to Florida and Missouri
HARDINESS: USDA Zones 3–9
SIZE: 6'–15' tall or more and as wide

INTEREST: Deciduous clumps of gray-barked stems, with dark green foliage. Female plants bear ¼" bright red berries in late summer to fall.
LIGHT CONDITIONS: Full sun to partial shade
SOIL/MOISTURE: Moisture-retentive, acid, fertile to average soil

DESCRIPTION: This shrub has recently become popular as an ornamental, and many new cultivars and hybrids have been released. A male plant is necessary to pollinate the females for good fruit production. Winterberry makes a fine specimen plant if kept pruned to shape, but is excellent massed in shaded, wet, or swampy areas, where it provides good cover and nesting sites for red-winged blackbirds, as well as food for many species including robins, brown thrashers, and mockingbirds. In some winters the berries are stripped before New Year's Day, but in other years the birds leave them until spring.

OPUNTIA SPP.

PRONUNCIATION: o-PUN-tee-a
COMMON NAME: Prickly pear
HOMELAND: Deserts, roadsides, and dry banks of North and South America
HARDINESS: USDA Zones 3–10 by species
SIZE: 6'–12' tall; 2'–6' across by species

INTEREST: Rounded flat, broad joints or pads, adorned with often colorful spines of all sizes; mostly solitary flowers and fleshy fruits
LIGHT CONDITIONS: Full sun
SOIL/MOISTURE: Loam, high in minerals and nutrient salts

DESCRIPTION: This genus consists of 200 or so species, many of them with interesting architectural forms and shapes. The succulent, flattened pads or joints (stems) are covered with clusters of large and small spines (reduced leaves) which emerge from areoles. The showy flowers, which are yellow, orange, purple, or white, are cup-shaped with a central boss of stamens; abundant edible fruits, usually rosy red in color, follow. These sweet, succulent fruits are a welcome source of food for fruit-eating mammals, reptiles, and birds. In the landscape they are appropriate for rock gardens and for difficult, exposed banks.

RHUS TYPHINA 'LACINIATA'

PRONUNCIATION: ROOS ty-FIN-ee-a
lass-INN-ee-ah-ta

COMMON NAME: Cutleaf staghorn sumac

HOMELAND: Along roadsides and field margins from Quebec to Ontario, south to Georgia, Indiana, and Iowa; cultivar of garden origin

HARDINESS: USDA Zones 3–8

SIZE: 15'–25' tall and as wide

INTEREST: Ferny foliage, crimson in fall. Dense clusters of whitish flowers in summer followed by crimson conelike fruit clusters.

LIGHT CONDITIONS: Full sun to light shade

SOIL/MOISTURE: Best in well-drained, average to poor, even dry soil

DESCRIPTION: This spreading shrub has hairy, sticky stems that are velvety when young. Its deeply cut, compound foliage turns brilliant red-crimson before dropping in fall. The species has male and female on separate plants (dioecious), but this cultivar is female and must be propagated vegetatively. The species is a valuable food source for many bird species including cardinals, cedar waxwings, mockingbirds, catbirds, wild turkeys, and ruffed grouse. Excellent as a specimen or in transition areas. The plant is short-lived, but often young shoots appear from runners that can be encouraged to replace declining adults.

RUBUS ODORATUS

PRONUNCIATION: ROO-bus o-dor-AH-tus

COMMON NAME: Thimbleberry, flowering raspberry

HOMELAND: Nova Scotia to Georgia

HARDINESS: USDA Zones 2–8

SIZE: 6'–9' tall; 6' or so across

INTEREST: Maplelike foliage with purplish pink, 2" flowers in early summer. Red fruits in late summer.

LIGHT CONDITIONS: Light to partial shade

SOIL/MOISTURE: Well-drained, rich soil

DESCRIPTION: Thimbleberries make colonies of dense, but not thorny, deciduous shrubs, which provide cover and nesting sites as well as food for flycatchers, mockingbirds, and catbirds. Many other species, including blue jays and some woodpeckers, feed on the fruit. The fragrant flowers are arranged in clusters among the large leaves, which are white-felted beneath. Useful in a shrub collection, especially to attract birds.

Sambucus canadensis
(American elderberry)

Vaccinium corymbosum
(high-bush blueberry)

Viburnum trilobum
(American cranberry
bush viburnum)

LEFT
Smilacina stellata
(starflower)

SAMBUCUS CANADENSIS

PRONUNCIATION: sam-BEW-kus
can-a DEN-sis

COMMON NAME: American elderberry

HOMELAND: Widespread in damp, open
places from Nova Scotia to Manitoba and
south to Florida and Texas

HARDINESS: USDA Zones 3–9

SIZE: 6'–12' tall; 6'–8' across

INTEREST: Large, pinnately compound leaves
turn greenish yellow in fall. Flat, showy clusters of fragrant cream flowers in early summer, followed by blue-black fruits.

LIGHT CONDITIONS: Full sun to light shade

SOIL/MOISTURE: Average soil, best where
moisture is plentiful

DESCRIPTION: American elderberry suckers readily and must be pruned regularly
to maintain a specimen shape. It is superb massed as a hedge or thicket, where it
is a valuable source of food and cover for mockingbirds, gray catbirds, and yellow warblers, who also use it for nesting. Numerous other bird species, including wild turkeys, woodpeckers, and thrushes, also eat the sweet berries. The fruit
was valued by Native Americans for making jellies and juice high in vitamin C.
Homemade elderberry and elderflower (elderblow) wines were popular drinks
in Colonial times.

SMILACINA STELLATA

PRONUNCIATION: smy-la-SEE-na stel-LAH-ta

COMMON NAME: Starflower, starbead

HOMELAND: Gravelly thickets and meadows
from Newfoundland to British Columbia,
south to New Jersey and west to Kansas, New
Mexico and Southern California

HARDINESS: USDA Zones 2–9

SIZE: 1'–2' tall; 1' across

INTEREST: Stem-clasping, broad 6" lanceolate
leaves; in late spring, terminal 2" long
racemes of creamy ¼" flowers, and striped
green berries appear

LIGHT CONDITIONS: Partial to light shade

SOIL/MOISTURE: Neutral to slightly acid
moist, fertile soil, enriched with humus

DESCRIPTION: Starflower colonizes readily by underground rhizomes but is not
invasive. Excellent in moist woodland gardens with ferns, foamflowers, lung-
worts, and columbines. The erect stems carry 6 or more handsome, channeled
leaves; the crowded inflorescence consists of 15–20 starry flowers. The common name starbead refers to the berries, which are striped in a star pattern with
brown or maroon; they mature to blackish red and provide food for birds and
small mammals.

VACCINIUM CORYMBOSUM

PRONUNCIATION: vax-IN-ee-um ko-rym-bo-sum

COMMON NAME: High-bush blueberry

HOMELAND: Woods, forest clearings, and bog communities from Maine to Florida and Louisiana

HARDINESS: USDA Zones 4–8

SIZE: 5′–6′ tall; 5′–6′ across

INTEREST: A profusion of urn-shaped ¼″ white flowers in spring, blue-green, oval leaves. Blue edible fruits; brilliant red fall color.

LIGHT CONDITIONS: Full sun to light shade

SOIL/MOISTURE: Damp, acid, sandy soil

DESCRIPTION: High-bush blueberry grows in open, damp areas, where it makes large stands; it is spectacular in the fall with an array of foliage colors—yellow, scarlet to crimson. This valuable food crop and cover plant for birds is also the source of the economic fruit crop. Cultivated fruits may grow ¾″ across. Low-bush blueberry, *V. angustifolium*, is a food crop in Maine, but should be used as an ornamental ground-covering shrub for acidic, moist soils.

VIBURNUM TRILOBUM

PRONUNCIATION: vi-BUR-num try-LOW-bum

COMMON NAME: American cranberry bush viburnum

HOMELAND: Moist woods from New Brunswick to British Columbia, south to New York, Michigan, South Dakota and Oregon

HARDINESS: USDA Zones 2–8

SIZE: 8′–12′ tall and as wide

INTEREST: Flat, 3″–4″ clusters of small white flowers in spring, followed by scarlet-orange berries; foliage turns yellow then red-maroon in fall

LIGHT CONDITIONS: Sun to part shade

SOIL/MOISTURE: Well-drained, moist soil

DESCRIPTION: This deciduous shrub has an attractive rounded shape, with upright or arching branches, clothed with 5″-long maplelike leaves. The clusters of fertile flowers are ringed by larger, sterile ones. The ¼″ berries mostly persist through the winter, although some are consumed by wildlife, particularly eastern bluebirds and cardinals. Wild turkeys, ring-necked pheasants, and grouse use American cranberry bush viburnum for cover as well as food. It is an excellent all-season landscape plant, especially valuable as a screening or hedge plant.

Appendix

Mail-Order Nurseries

Adamgrove Nursery
Route 1, Box 246
California, MO 65018
*Hemerocallis, irises,
peonies. Catalog: $3*

Alpen Gardens
173 Lawrence Lane
Kalispell, MT
59901-4633
(406) 257-2540
Dahlia tubers

Jacques Amand, Bulb
  Specialists
PO Box 59001
Potomac, MD 20859
(800) 452-5414
*Spring and summer blooming
bulbs*

Ambergate Gardens
8730 County Rd. 43
Chaska, MN 55318
(612) 443-2248
*Hostas, unusual perennials,
Martagon lilies. Catalog: $2*

Anderson Iris Gardens
22179 Keather Ave. N.
Forest Lake, MN 55025
(612) 433-5268
*Bearded iris, peonies.
Catalog: $1*

Antique Rose Emporium
9300 Lueckemeyer
Brenham, TX 77833
(409) 836-9051
Old garden roses. Catalog: $5

Antonelli Brothers, Inc.
2545 Capitola Rd.
Santa Cruz, CA 95062
(408) 475-5222
*Tuberous begonias, fuchsias.
Catalog: $1*

Appalachian Gardens
PO Box 82
Waynesboro, PA 17268
(717) 762-4312
*Conifers, flowering
shrubs, trees.*

Arborvillage Farm
  Nursery
PO Box 227
Holt, MO 64048
(816) 264-3911
Shrubs, trees. Catalog: $1

Arrowhead Alpines
PO Box 857
Flowerville, MI 48836
(517) 223-3581
*Conifers, wildflowers, ferns,
alpines. Catalog: $2*

Arrowhead Nursery
5030 Watia Rd.
Bryson City, NC
28713-9683
*Trees, shrubs native to
Southeast. List*

B & D Lilies
330 P St.
Port Townsend, WA
98368
(360) 385-1738 *Lilies.
Catalog: $3*

Bio-Quest International
1781 Glen Oak Dr.
Santa Barbara, CA
93108
(805) 969-4072
Rare Clivia, amaryllis
hybrids

Bluestone Perennials
7211 Middle Ridge Rd.
Madison, OH 44057
(800) 852-5243
Herbaceous perennials, shrubs

Borbeleta Gardens
15980 Canby Ave.
Fairbault, MN 55021
(507) 334-2807
Iris, Hemerocallis,
Asiatic lilies. Catalog: $3

The Bovees Nursery
1737 SW Coronado
Portland, OR 97219
(503) 244-9341
Flowering shrubs, trees,
perennials, vines, tropical
rhododendrons. Catalog: $2

Bonnie Brae Gardens
1105 SE Christensen Rd.
Corbett, OR 97019
(503) 695-5190
Daffodils. List: send long
SASE

Brand Peony Farm
PO Box 842
Saint Cloud, MN
56302
Peonies, especially heirloom
varieties. Catalog: $1

Briarwood Gardens
14 Gully Lane
East Sandwich, MA
02537
Rhododendrons. Catalog: $1

Brown's Kalmia and
  Azalea Nursery
8527 Semiahmoo Dr.
Blaine, WA 98230
(360) 371-5551
Kalmia, azaleas. List: $1

Busse Gardens
13579 Tenth St., NW
Cokato, MN
55321-9426
(320) 286-2654
Herbaceous perennials,
Hemerocallis, *hostas, iris,*
peonies. Catalog: $2

Cactus by Dodie
934 Mettler Rd.
Lodi, CA 95242
(209) 368-3692
Cacti and succulents.
Catalog: $2

California Carnivores
7020 Trenton-
Healdsburg Rd.
Forestville, CA 95436
(707) 838-1630
Carnivorous plants.
Catalog: $2

Camellia Forest Nursery
125 Carolina Forest Rd.
Chapel Hill, NC 27516
Conifers, flowering shrubs,
trees, some herbaceous plants,
camellias. Catalog: $2

Campanula Connoisseur
702 Traver Trail
Glenwood Springs, CO
81601
Campanula. Catalog: $1

Caprice Nursery
15425 Southwest
Pleasant Hill Rd.
Sherwood, OR 97140
(503) 625-7241
Peonies, Japanese and
Siberian irises,
Hemerocallis, Hostas.
Catalog: $2

Carroll Gardens
PO Box 310
Westminster, MD
21158
(410) 848-5422
Flowering shrubs, trees,
herbaceous perennials, grasses,
hardy ferns. Catalog: $3

Cascade Daffodils
PO Box 10626
White Bear Lake, MN
55110-0626
(612) 426-9616
Collector's miniature and
standard daffodils.
Catalog: $2

Cascade Forestry
  Nursery
22033 Fillmore Rd.
Cascade, IA 52033
(319) 852-3042
Conifers, shrubs, and trees

Christa's Cactus
529 West Pima
Coolidge, AZ 85228
(520) 723-4185
Desert trees, shrubs, succulents, cacti. Catalog: $1

Collector's Nursery
16804 NE 102d Ave.
Battle Ground, WA
98604
(360) 574-3832
Unusual conifers, flowering shrubs, trees, herbaceous perennials, vines, alpines, dwarf conifers, Gentiana, Tricyrtis, species Iris. Catalog: $2

Colorado Alpines, Inc.
PO Box 2708
Avon, CO 81620
(970) 949-6464
Dwarf conifers, alpines, native shrubs, trees, plants of the west

Companion Plants
7247 North Coolville Ridge Rd.
Athens, OH 45701
(614) 592-4643
Woodland plants, perennials, herbs, scented geraniums. Catalog: $3

The Compleat Garden Clematis Nursery
217 Argilla Rd.
Ipswich, MA 01938-2617
(508) 356-3197
Clematis. Catalog: $3

Cooley's Gardens
PO Box 126
Silverton, OR 97381
(503) 873-5463
Bearded iris. Catalog: $5

Cooper's Garden
2345 Decatur Ave.
N. Golden Valley, MN 55427
(612) 591-0495
Herbaceous perennials, Iris. Catalog: $1

Country Bloomers Nursery
RR 2
Udall, KS 67146
(316) 986-5518
Old garden roses, miniatures, some modern roses. List: send long SASE

Country Cottage
Route 2, Box 130
Sedgwick, KS 67135
Groundcover succulents. List: send long SASE

Cricket Hill Garden
670 Walnut Hill Rd.
Thomaston, CT 06787
(860) 283-1042
Chinese tree peonies. Catalog: $2

Crownsville Nursery
PO Box 797
Crownsville, MD 21032
(410) 849-3143
Woody plants, herbaceous perennials, grasses, ferns, Hemerocallis, hostas. Catalog: $2

The Cummins Garden
22 Robertsville Rd.
Marlboro, NJ 07746
(732) 536-2591
Dwarf conifers, Rhododendron, azalea, Pieris, Kalmia, heathers. Catalog: $2

Cycad Gardens
4524 Toland Way
Los Angeles, CA 90041
(213) 255-6651
Cycads. List: send long SASE

Daffodil Mart
Route 3, Box 794
Gloucester, VA 23061
(804) 693-6339
Vast list of Narcissus varieties; also tulips, crocuses, alliums, bulbs. Catalog: $1

Desert Nursery
1301 S. Copper St.
Deming, NM 88030
(505) 546-6264
Succulents and hardy cacti. List: send long SASE

Desert Theatre
17 Behler Rd.
Watsonville, CA 95076
(408) 728-5513
South American and African succulents and cacti. Catalog: $2

Dooley Gardens
212 North High Dr.
Hutchinson, MN 55350
(320) 587-3050
Chrysanthemums

Jim Duggan Flower
  Nursery
1452 Santa Fe Dr.
Encinitas, CA 92024
(619) 943-1658
South African bulbs.
Catalog: $2

Eastern Plant Specialties
PO Box 226
Georgetown, ME
04548
(207) 371-2888
Dwarf conifers, flowering
shrubs, trees, Kalmia,
Rhododendron, *azalea.*
Catalog: $2

Fairweather Gardens
PO Box 330
Sheppards Mill Rd.
Greenwich, NJ 08323
(609) 451-6261
Woody plants, flowering
shrubs and trees

Fancy Fronds
PO Box 1090
Gold Bar, WA 98251
Hardy and temperate ferns,
many new introductions.
Catalog: $2

Field House Alpines
6730 W. Mercer Way
Mercer Island, WA
98040
Alpine and rock garden
seeds. Catalog: $2

Fieldstone Gardens
620 Quaker Lane
Vassalboro, ME
04989-9713
(207) 923-3836
Herbaceous perennials, herbs,
alpines, groundcovers.
Catalog: $2

Foliage Gardens
2003 128th Avenue SE
Bellevue, WA 98005
(206) 747-2998
Ferns and dwarf Japanese
maple cultivars. Catalog: $2

Forest Farm
990 Tetherow Rd.
Williams, OR
97544-9599
Conifers, flowering shrubs,
trees, herbaceous plants.
Catalog: $3

Fox Hill Farm
434 W. Michigan Ave.
Parma, MI
49269-0009
(517) 531-3179
Herbs, scented geraniums

The Fragrant Path
PO Box 328
Fort Calhoun, NE
68023
Fragrant perennials, annu-
als, herbs, vines (rare and
heirloom). Catalog: $2

Garden Place
PO Box 388
Mentor, OH
44061-0388
(216) 255-3705
Groundcovers, perennials,
grasses. Catalog: $1

Gilson Gardens
3059 U.S. Route 20
PO Box 277
Perry, OH 44081
(216) 259-5252
Low-growing shrubs, peren-
nials, vines, and sedums

Girard Nurseries
PO Box 428
Geneva, OH 44041
(216) 466-2881
Conifers, flowering shrubs,
trees, groundcovers, perenni-
als, vines

Glasshouse Works
  Greenhouses
Church St.
PO Box 97
Stewart, OH
45778-0097
(614) 662-2142
Tropical and subtropical
plants, ferns, succulents,
shrubs, trees, dwarf conifers,
tender and hardy perennials,
variegated plants.
Catalog: $2

Goodwin Creek Gardens
PO Box 83
Williams, OR 97544
(541) 846-7357
*Herbs, fragrant plants, plants
for hummingbirds and butterflies. Catalog: $1*

Gossler Farms Nursery
1200 Weaver Rd.
Springfield, OR
97478-9691
(541) 746-3922
*Conifers, flowering shrubs,
trees, Hamamelis,
Magnolia, Rhododen-
dron. Catalog: $2*

The Gourd Garden
4808 E. Country Rd.
30-A
Santa Rosa Beach, FL
32459
(904) 231-2007
*Gourd and herb seed. List:
send long SASE*

The Green Escape
PO Box 1417
Palm Harbor, FL 34682
(813) 784-1991
*Rare and uncommon palms
for the conservatory and cold
hardy. Catalog: $6*

GreenLady Gardens
aka Skittone Bulbs
1415 Eucalyptus
San Francisco, CA
94132
(415) 753-3332
*Wide variety of species and
bulbs. Catalog: $3*

Greenmantle Nursery
3010 Ettersburg Rd.
Garberville, CA 95440
(707) 986-7504
*Old Garden roses. List: send
long SASE*

Greer Gardens
1280 Goodpasture
Island Rd.
Eugene, OR
97401-1794
*Conifers, flowering shrubs,
trees, perennials, grasses, ferns,
bonsai plants, azalea,
Rhododendron.
Catalog: $3*

Grigsby Cactus Gardens
2326-2354 Bella Vista
Dr.
Vista, CA 92084-7836
(760) 727-1323
*Rare succulents and cacti.
Catalog: $2*

Heard Gardens, Ltd.
5355 Merle Hay Rd.
Johnston, IA 50131
(515) 276-4533
Lilacs. Catalog: $2

Heaths and Heathers
E. 502 Haskell Hill Rd.
Shelton, WA
98584-8429
(360) 427-5318
*Heaths and heathers. List: send
long SASE*

Heirloom Garden Seeds
PO Box 138
Guerneville, CA 95446
*Herbs and heirloom flowers.
Catalog: $2.50*

Heirloom Old Garden
Roses
24062 NE Riverside Dr.
St. Paul, OR 97137
(503) 538-1576
*Old garden and English roses.
Catalog: $5*

Heritage Rose Gardens
16831 Mitchell Creek Dr.
Fort Bragg, CA
95437-8727
(707) 964-3748
*Old garden roses.
Catalog: $1.50*

Heronswood Nursery
7530 288th St. NE
Kingston, WA 98346
(206) 297-4172
*Conifers, flowering shrubs,
trees, herbaceous plants.
Catalog: $3*

High Country Rosarium
1717 Downing St.
Denver, CO 80209
(303) 832-4026
*Old garden roses, roses
for a variety of conditions.
Catalog: $1*

Hildenbrandt's Iris
  Gardens
1710 Cleveland St.
Lexington, NE
68850-2721
(308) 324-4334
*Hostas, peonies, bearded iris,
poppies. List: send long SASE*

Holly Haven Hybrids
136 Sanwood Rd.
Knoxville, TN
37923-5564
*Hollies. List: send long
SASE*

Holly Lane Iris
  Gardens
10930 Holly Lane
Osseo, MN 55369
(612) 420-4876
*Bearded iris, Siberian iris,
peonies, Hemerocallis,
Hosta*

Hollyvale Farm
PO Box 434
Hoquiam, WA 98520
Hollies. Catalog: $5

J. L. Hudson,
Seedsman
PO Box 1058
Redwood City, CA
94064
*No phone. No visits. Seeds
only—but seeds of just
about everything from all
over the world. Catalog: $1*

Huff's Garden Mums
PO Box 187
Burlington, KS 66839-
0187
(800) 279-4675
Chrysanthemums

Intermountain Cactus
2344 S. Redwood Rd.
Salt Lake City, UT
84119
(801) 966-7176
*Hardy cactus. List: send long
SASE*

Iris Country
6219 Topaz St. NE
Brooks, OR 97305
(503) 393-4739, 6:00
A.M. or eves., PST
*Iris: beardless, species, his-
toric bearded, modern ultra-
hardy bearded.
Catalog: $1.50*

Iris Test Gardens
James and Janet Leifer
1102 Endicott-
  St. John Rd.
St. John, WA 99171
(509) 648-3873
*Unusual bearded iris.
Catalog: $1*

Ivies of the World
PO Box 408
Weirsdale, FL
32195-0408
(352) 821-2201
Ivy. Catalog: $2

Joy Creek Nursery
20300 NW Watson Rd.
Scappoose, OR 97056
(503) 543-7474
*Shrubs, herbaceous perenni-
als, alpines, grasses.
Catalog: $2*

Kartuz Greenhouses
1408 Sunset Dr.
Vista, CA 92083-6531
(619) 941-3613
*Tropical and subtropical
plants, such as begonias,
Gesneriad, Passiflora.
Catalog: $2*

Kelleygreen Rhodo-
  dendron Nursery
185 Roaring Camp Ln.
Drain, OR 97435
(541) 836-2290
*Rhododendron, Japanese
maples, azalea, Pieris, and
Kalmia. Catalog: $1.25*

Kelly's Plant World
10266 E. Princeton
Sanger, CA 93657
(209) 294-7676
*Rare and unusual plants,
summer-blooming bulbs,
Canna, Lycoris,
Crinum, also trees and
shrubs. Catalog: $1*

Klehm Nursery
4210 N. Duncan Rd.
Champagne, IL 61821
(800) 553-3715
*Herbaceous perennials,
ferns, Siberian iris,
Hemerocallis, hostas,
peonies. Catalog: $4*

Lamb Nurseries
Route 1, Box 460B
Longbeach, WA 98631
(360) 642-4856
Alpines and perennials, also groundcovers, succulents, vines, and flowering shrubs.
Catalog: $2

Lamtree Farm
2323 Copeland Rd.
Warrensville, NC 28693
(910) 385-6144
Native propagated trees and shrubs: Franklinia, Stewartia, Styrax, Halesia, Rhododendron, *azalea,* Kalmia. *Catalog: $2*

Landscape Alternatives
1705 St. Alban's St.
Rooksville, MN 55113
(612) 488-3142
Native U.S. wildflowers.
Growing Guide: $2

Las Pilitas Nursery
3232 Las Pilitas Rd.
Santa Margarita, CA 93453
(805) 438-5992
California native plants, plants for special conditions.
Catalog: $8 (price list is free)

Lilypons Water Gardens
6800 Lilypons Rd.
PO Box 10
Buckeystown, MD 21717-0010
(301) 874-5133
Aquatic plants. Catalog: $5

Logee's Greenhouses
141 North St.
Danielson, CT 06239
(860) 774-8038
Tropical and subtropical shrubs, vines, tender perennials, begonias, geraniums

Louisiana Nursery
5853 Highway 182
Opelousas, LA 70570
(318) 948-3696
Catalogs:
$6 Magnolias, perennials, and woody plants
$4 Iris and Hemerocallis
$5 Crinum and other rare bulbs
$4 Fruiting trees, shrubs, and vines
$4 Hydrangea
$4 Bamboos and ornamental grasses
$3 Clivia list
$29.50 for all

Lowe's Own-Root Roses
6 Sheffield Rd.
Nashua, NH 03062-3028
(603) 888-2214
Old garden roses, shrubs, climbers, ramblers, and custom grafted. Catalog: $3

Mad River Imports
PO Box 1685
Fayston, VT 05660
(802) 496-3004
Spring and summer blooming bulbs

Maple Tree Gardens
PO Box 547
Ponca, NE 68770-0547
(402) 755-2615
Maple trees, bearded iris, Hemerocallis, Hosta.
Catalog: $1

Maryland Aquatic Nurseries
3427 N. Furnace Rd.
Jarrettsville, MD 21084
(410) 557-7615
Aquatic and waterside plants.
Catalog: $2

Mary's Plant Farm
2410 Lanes Mill Rd.
Hamilton, OH 45013
(513) 892-2055
Flowering shrubs, perennials, ferns, iris, grasses, native plants. Catalog: $1

Mendocino Heirloom Roses
PO Box 670
Mendocino, CA 95460
(707) 937-0963
Antique, species, and unusual roses. Catalog: $1

Midwest Cactus
PO Box 163
New Melle, MO 63365
(314) 828-5389
Hardy cacti, sedums, and yuccas. Catalog: $2

Mileager's Gardens
4838 Douglas Ave.
Racine, WI
53402-2498
(414) 639-2371
*Roses, herbaceous perennials,
vines, grasses. Catalog: $1*

Miniature Plant
  Kingdom
4125 Harrison Grade
  Rd.
Sebastopol, CA 95472
(707) 874-2233
*Dwarf conifers, bonsai suit-
able trees and shrubs, miniature roses, some perennials
and alpines. Catalog: $2.50*

Mountain Maples
PO Box 1329
54561 Registrar's
  Guest Rd.
Laytonville, CA
95454-1329
(707) 984-6522
*Japanese and other maples.
Catalog: $2*

Mount Tahoma
  Nursery
28111 112th Ave.
E. Graham, WA 98338
(206) 847-9827
*Small shrubs, and primarily
alpines. Catalog: $1*

Nature's Curiosity
  Shop
3551 Evening Canyon
  Rd.
Oceanside, CA 92056
*Variegated plants, succulents.
Catalog: $1*

Neon Palm Nursery
3525 Stony Point Rd.
Santa Rosa, CA 95407
(707) 585-8100
*Subtropical palms and
cycads. Catalog: $1*

New Peony Farm
PO Box 18235
St. Paul, MN 55118
(612) 457-8994
Peonies

Niche Gardens
1111 Dawson Rd.
Chapel Hill, NC
27516
(919) 967-0078
*Natives of the southeastern
U.S. Catalog: $3*

Nichol's Garden
  Nursery, Inc.
1190 N. Pacific Hwy.
Albany, OR 97321
(541) 928-9280
Herbs, mints

Nurseries at North
  Glen
Route 2 Box 2700
Glen Saint Mary, FL
32040
(904) 259-2754
Hardy palms and cycads

Oakes Daylillies
8204 Monday Rd.
Corryton, TN 37721
(423) 687-3770
Hemerocallis

Oikos Tree Crops
PO Box 19425
Kalamazoo, MI
49019-0425
(616) 624-6233
*Fruit and nut trees, oaks.
Catalog: $1*

Old House Gardens
536 Third St.
Ann Arbor, MI
48103-4957
(313) 995-1486
Heirloom bulbs. Catalog: $1

Orgel's Orchids
18950 Southwest
  136th St.
Miami, FL
33196-1942
(305) 233-7168
*Carnivorous plants. List:
send long SASE*

Peter Pauls Nurseries
4665 Chapin Rd.
Canandaigua, NY
14424-8713
(716) 394-7397
Carnivorous plants

Perennial Pleasures
  Nursery
2 Brick House Rd.
East Hardwick, VT
05836
(802) 472-5104
*Perennials and herbs for his-
toric restoration plantings.
Catalog: $2*

Piccadilly Farm 1971
Whippoorwill Rd.
Bishop, GA 30621
(706) 769-6516
Hosta, Helleborus
Catalog: $1

Plant Delights Nursery
9241 Sauls Rd.
Raleigh, NC 27603
(919) 772-4794
*Conifers, flowering shrubs,
herbaceous perennials, grasses,
hostas. Catalog: $2*

Plants of the Southwest
Agua Fria
Route 6, Box 11A
Santa Fe, NM 87505
(505) 438-8888
*Flowering shrubs, trees, herba-
ceous perennials, vegetables,
herbs, xerophytes, penstemons.
Catalog: $3.50*

Plants of the Wild
PO Box 866
Tekoa, WA 99033
(509) 284-2848
*Natives of the Pacific
Northwest. Catalog: $1*

Pond Doctor
HC 65, Box 265
Kingston, AR 72742
(501) 665-2232
Aquatic plants. Catalog: $2

Prairie Moon Nursery
Route 3, Box 163
Winona, MN 55987
(507) 452-5231
*Native plants of midwest U.S.
Catalog: $2*

Prairie Nursery
PO Box 306
Westfield, WI 53964
(608) 296-3679
*Native perennials and grasses
of the U.S. prairie*

Primrose Path
R.D. 2, Box 110
Scottdale, PA 15683
(412) 887-6756
*Herbaceous perennials, alpines.
Catalog: $2*

Quality Plants
6792 Buell Rd.
Igo, CA 96047
(916) 467-3426
*Succulents and Lewesia
species. Catalog*

Rare Conifer Nursery
PO Box 100
Potter Valley, CA
95469
Conifers

Rare Plant Research
9527 Southeast Wichita
Milwaukee, OR 97222
*Rare succulents. List: send
long SASE*

Rarifolia
Kintnersville, PA 18930
(215) 847-8208
*Dwarf conifers, Japanese
maples. Catalog: $3*

Reath's Nursery
County Rd. 577N-195
Vulcan, MI 49892
(906) 563-9777
Peonies. Catalog: $2

Riverdale Iris Gardens
PO Box 524
Rockford, MN 55373
(612) 477-4859
*Siberian, hardy dwarf, tall,
and bearded iris. Catalog: $1*

Robinett Bulb Farm
PO Box 1306
Sebastopol, CA
95473-1306
*West coast native bulbs:
Allium, Brodiaea,
Calochortus, others
List: send long SASE*

Rocknoll Nursery
7812 Mad River Rd.
Hillsboro, OH 45133
(614) 454-3018
*Alpines, rock, and U.S.
natives. Catalog: $1*

Rock Spray Nursery
PO Box 693
Truro, MA 02666
(508) 349-6769
*Heaths and heathers.
Catalog: $2*

Rocky Mountain Rare
  Plants
PO Box 200483
Denver, CO
80220-0483
*Seeds only, alpines.
Catalog: $1*

Roses of Yesterday and
Today
802 Brown's Valley Rd.
Watsonville, CA
95076-0398
(408) 724-3537
*Old garden roses, hybrid
teas. Catalog: $4*

Roslyn Nursery
211 Burrs Lane
Dix Hills, NY 11746
(516) 643-9347
*Conifers, flowering shrubs,
trees, herbaceous perennials,
hostas, ferns, azalea,
Rhododendron,
Kalmia, Pieris,
Viburnum, Camellia,
Ilex. Catalog: $3*

Russell Graham
4030 Eagle Crest Rd.
NW
Salem, OR 97304
(503) 362-1135
*Shrubs, perennials, ferns.
Catalog: $2*

Sandy Mush Herb
Nursery
316 Surrett Cove Rd.
Leicester, NC
28748-5517
(704) 683-2014
*Flowering shrubs, trees,
perennials, and herbs.
Catalog: $5*

Savory's Gardens, Inc.
5300 Whiting Ave.
Edina, MN 55439
(612) 941-8755
*Perennials, shade plants,
Hemerocallis, Hosta.
Catalog: $2*

John Scheepers, Inc.
PO Box 700
Bantam, CT 06750
(860) 567-0838
*Large selection of bulbs,
standard varieties. Catalog:
free with $25 minimum
order*

Schreiner's Gardens
3625 Quinaby Rd. NE
Salem, OR 97303
(503) 393-3232
Iris. Catalog: $5

Seeds of Change
1364 Rufina Circle #5
Santa Fe, NM 87501
*Vegetable and annuals, heir-
loom varieties. Catalog: $3*

Select Seeds
180 Stickney Rd.
Union, CT
06076-4617
(860) 684-9310
*Old-fashioned flowers and
seeds. Catalog: $1*

Sevald Nursery
4937 Third Ave. S.
Minneapolis, MN
55409
(612) 822-3279
*Herbaceous peonies.
Catalog: $2*

Shady Oaks Nursery
112 Tenth Ave. SE
Waseca, MN 56093
(507) 835-5033
*Shrubs, herbaceous perenni-
als, hostas, native plants,
ferns, groundcovers for shade.
Catalog: $2.50*

Shein's Cactus
3360 Drew St.
Marina, CA 93933
(408) 384-7765
*Cactus and succulents.
Catalog: $1*

Shooting Star Nursery
444 Bates Rd.
Frankfort, KY 40601
(502) 233-1679
*Native shrubs, trees, herba-
ceous perennials, grasses*

Siskiyou Rare Plant
Nursery
2825 Cummings Rd.
Medford, OR 97501
(541) 772-6846
*Dwarf conifers; dwarf
shrubs and trees; alpine rock,
woodland plants; hardy
ferns. Catalog: $3*

Stallings Nursery
910 Encinitas Blvd.
Encinitas, CA 92024
(619) 753-3079
*Tropical and subtropical
plants. Catalog: $3*

Story House Herb Farm
Route 7, Box 246
Murray, KY 42071
(502) 753-4158
Herbs. Catalog: $2

Sunlight Gardens, Inc.
174 Golden Lane
Andersonville, TN
37705
(423) 494-8237
Trees, flowering shrubs, herba-
ceous perennials, ferns—
native to eastern North
America. Catalog: $3

Sunnybrook Farms
Nursery
9448 Mayfield Rd.
Chesterland, OH 44026
(216) 729-7232
Herbs, perennials, ivies, and
hostas. Catalog: $2

Sunnyslope Gardens
8638 Huntington Dr.
San Gabriel, CA 91775
(818) 287-4071
Chrysanthemums

Sunshine Farm and
Gardens
Route 5
Renick, WV 24966
(304) 497-3163
Very rare and exceptional
plants. List: send long SASE

Swan Island Dahlias
PO Box 700
Canby, OR 97013
(503) 266-7711
Dahlias. Catalog: $3

Thompson and Morgan
PO Box 1308
Jackson, NJ
08527-0308
(908) 363-2225
Mostly seeds, some plants

Tranquil Lake Nursery
45 River St.
Rehobeth, MA
02769-1359
Hemerocallis, Japanese and
Siberian iris. Catalog: $1

Transplant Nursery
1586 Parkertown Rd.
Lavonia, GA 30553
(706) 356-8947
Southeastern U.S. natives,
Rhododendron,
Camellia, chiefly Azalea.
Catalog: $1

William Tricker, Inc.
7125 Tanglewood Dr.
Independence, OH
44131
(216) 524-3491
Aquatic plants, dwarf water
lilies. Catalog: $2

Van Engelen, Inc.
23 Tulip Dr.
Bantam, CT 06750
(860) 567-8734
Bulbs

Andre Viette Farm and
Nursery
State Rd. 608
Longmeadow Rd.
Fisherville, VA 22939
(540) 943-2315
Flowering shrubs, herbaceous
perennials, ferns, grasses,
Hemerocallis, hostas, iris,
peonies. Catalog: $5

Washington Evergreen
Nursery
PO Box 388
Leicester, NC 28748
(704) 683-4518
(April–October)
(803) 747-1641
(November–March)
Dwarf shrubs, rhododendrons,
dwarf conifers, Kalmia.
Catalog: $2

Waterford Gardens
74 East Allendale Rd.
Saddle River, NJ 07458
(201) 327-0721 or
327-0337
Aquatic plants, water lilies,
lotuses. Catalog: $5

Waushara Gardens
North 5491 Fifth Dr.
Plainfield, WI 54966
(715) 335-4462
Gladiolus, Asiatic lilies.
Catalog: $1

Wayside Gardens
1 Garden Lane
Hodges, SC
29695-0001
(800) 845-1124
*Perennials, flowering
shrubs, trees*

Wedge Nursery
Route 2, Box 114
Albert Lea, MN 56007
(507) 373-5225
Lilacs

We-Du Nurseries
Route 5, Box 724
Marion, NC 28752
(704) 738-8300
*Southeastern native and
analogous Oriental wood-
land and rock plants; ferns,
species Iris, Trillium.
Catalog: $2*

Well-Sweep Herb
  Farm
205 Mt. Bethel Rd.
Port Murray, NJ
07865
(908) 852-5390
*Perennials, herbs, scented
geraniums. Catalog: $2*

White Flower Farm
Route 63
Litchfield, CT
 06759-0050
(800) 503-9624
*Perennials, flowering shrubs,
roses, vines. Catalog: $5*

White Rabbit Roses
PO Box 191
Elk, CA 95432
(707) 877-1888
Unusual roses

Wicklein's Water
  Gardens
PO Box 9780
Baldwin, MD 21013
(410) 823-1335
*Aquatic and bog plants.
Catalog: $2*

Gilbert H. Wild &
  Son, Inc.
PO Box 338
1112 Joplin St.
Sarcoxie, MO
64862-0338
(417) 548-3514
*Hemerocallis, iris,
peonies. Catalog: $3*

Nancy Wilson Species
  & Miniature Narcissus
6525 Briceland-Thorn
  Rd.
Garberville, CA 95542
(707) 923-2407
*Species and miniature daf-
fodils. Catalog: $1*

Windrose Nursery
1093 Mill Rd.
Pen Argyl, PA 18072
(610) 588-1037
*Oaks, woody plants, flower-
ing shrubs, and ornamental
trees. Catalog: $3*

Woodlanders, Inc.
1128 Colleton Ave.
Aiken, SC 29801
(803) 648-7522
*Conifers, flowering shrubs,
trees, herbaceous plants,
ferns. Catalog: $2*

Wrenwood of Berkeley
  Springs
Route 4, Box 361
Berkeley Springs, WV
25411
(304) 258-3071
*Perennials, sedums, rock
plants. Catalog: $2.50*

Guy Wrinkle Exotic
  Plants
11610 Addison St.
North Hollywood, CA
91601
(310) 670-8637
*Cycads, caudiciforms, succu-
lents. Catalog: $1*

Yucca Do Nursery
Rte. 3, Box 104
Hempstead, TX 77445
(409) 826-4580
*Texas and southeastern
natives and conifers,
flowering shrubs.
Catalog: $4*

Marsh marigold (*Caltha palustris*), 76

Meadow foam (*Limnanthes douglasii*), 32

Nodding mandarin (*Disporum maculatum*), 57

Nodding onion (*Allium cernuum*), 20

Northern sea oats (*Chasmanthium latifolium*), 24

Obedient plant (*Physostegia virginiana*), 41

Pink turtlehead (*Chelone lyonii*), 77

Pitcher plant (*Sarracenia purpurea*), 88

Prairie coneflower (*Ratibida pinnata*), 41

Prickly pear (*Opuntia* spp.), 104

Purple coneflower (*Echinacea purpurea*), 25

Royal fern (*Osmunda regalis*), 61

Rue anemone (*Anemonella thalictroides*), 52

Shooting star (*Dodecatheon meadia*), 57

Silverbell (*Halesia* spp.), 101

Skunk cabbage (*Symplocarpus foetidus*), 88

Sneezeweed (*Helenium autumnale*), 29

Spider lupine (*Lupinus benthamii*), 36

Split beard bluestem (*Andropogon ternarius*), 21

Starflower (*Smilacina stellata*), 108

Summersweet (*Clethra alnifolia*), 77

Swamp pink (*Helonias bullata*), 80

Swamp rose mallow (*Hibiscus moscheutos*), 81

Thimbleberry (*Rubus odoratus*), 105

Trillium (*Trillium grandiflorum*), 65

Turk's cap lily (*Lilium superbum*), 33

Twinleaf (*Jeffersonia diphylla*), 60

Virginia bluebells (*Mertensia virginica*), 60

Water lily (*Nymphaea odorata*), 85

Western skunk cabbage (*Lysichiton americanum*), 84

Wild ginger (*Asarum* spp.), 53

Wild hyacinth (*Camassia scilloides*), 53

Wild hydrangea (*Hydrangea arborescens*), 32

Winterberry (*Ilex verticillata*), 104

Wintergreen (*Gaultheria procumbens*), 100

Yellowroot (*Xanthorhiza simplicissima*), 69

Title page: *Trillium grandiflorum*. **Contents** page (clockwise from top left): mosses, ferns, *Clintonia umbellulata*; staghorn cholla (*Opuntia acanthocarpa*); boltonia (*Boltonia asteroides*); yellow pitcher plants (*Sarrancenia flava*). **p. 8:** garden coreopsis (*Coreopsis tinctoria*). **p. 11:** weeping Brewer spruce (*Picea brewerana*). **Plants for Meadow and Prairie** chapter opener (clockwise from top left): *Helenium amarum*; hardy ageratum, or mist flower (*Eupatorium coelestinum*); prairie blazing star (*Liatris pycnostachya*); red asclepias (*Asclpeias incarnata*); 'Gloriosa' daisy (*Rudbeckia hirta*); purple coneflower. **p. 16:** *Rudbeckia* 'Goldsturm'. **Wildflowers of the Woodland** chapter opener (clockwise from top left): *Anemone virginia; Dicentra eximia; Trillium cuneatum;* phlox and trillium. **p. 48:** pink-shell azalea (*Rhododendron vaseyi*). **Plants for the Water's Edge** chapter opener (clockwise from top left): *Gentiana andrewsii*; yellow pitcher plant (*Sarracenia flava*); buttonbush (*Cephalanthus occidentalis*); fern crosiers and skunk cabbages; sarracenias and tussock sedge (*Carex stricta*). **p. 72:** southern *Gaura lindheimeri*. **Berries, Pods, and Seeds for Ornament and Wildlife** chapter opener (clockwise from top left): forest floor; baneberry (*Actaea rubra*) and doll's-eyes (*A. pachypoda*); false Solomon's-seal (*Smilacina racemosa*); spikenard (*Aralia racemosa*); *Smilacina racemosa*; lowbush blueberry (*Vaccinium angustifolium*); American highbush cranberry (*Viburnum trilobum*). **p. 92:** foamflower (*Tiarella cordifolia*). **Appendix** opener (clockwise from top left): Northern California native flowers; blue false indigo (*Baptisia australis*); *Lonicera sempervirens* 'Sulphurea'; Canadian hemlock (*Tsuga canadensis*); orange asclepias (*A. tuberosa*); blue-flowered pickerelweed (*Pontederia cordata*) and arrow arum (*Peltandra virginica*); leather flower (*Clematis ochroleuca*); rattlesnake master (*Eryngium yuccifolium*).

U.S. Plant Hardiness Zones: Approximate range of average annual minimum temperatures (°F): zone 1: below -50°; zone 2: -50° to -40°; zone 3: -40° to -30°; zone 4: -30° to -20°; zone 5: -20° to -10°; zone 6: -10° to 0°; zone 7: 0° to 10°; zone 8: 10° to 20°; zone 9: 20° to 30°: zone 10: 30° to 40°